Learning ~~~~~~ the Etheric World

Empathy, the After-Image and a New Social Ethic

Baruch Luke Urieli
and
Hans Müller-Wiedemann

with source-material by Rudolf Steiner
and other authors compiled by
Thomas Stöckli

Mike Reiners
Feb. 5, 2002

TEMPLE LODGE
London

Translated by Simon Blaxland de Lange

Temple Lodge Publishing
51 Queen Caroline Street
London W6 9QL

www.templelodge.com

Published by Temple Lodge 1998
Reprinted 2000

Originally published in German under the title *Übungswege zur Erfahrung des Ätherischen, Empathie, Nachbild und neue Sozialethik* by Verlag am Goetheanum, Dornach, Switzerland in 1995

A catalogue record for this book is available from the British Library

ISBN 1 902636 00 7

Cover: art from *The Plant Between Sun and Earth*, reproduced by permission of Rudolf Steiner Press; design by S. Gulbekian
Typeset by DP Photosetting, Aylesbury, Bucks.
Printed and bound in Great Britain by Cromwell Press Limited, Trowbridge, Wiltshire

Contents

Foreword*
Baruch Luke Urieli

Mankind Crosses the Threshold

As I cast my eye over the modern world in both its wider and more intimate contexts, I find the clearest evidence for the threshold to the spiritual world having been crossed in the innumerable people who have begun to have conscious and semi-conscious experiences of the *etheric* world. Thus people today are with a part of their being—and for the most part not in a fully conscious way—entering a world in constant movement and flux. From this point of view the state of restlessness, rush and lack of time which so constantly threatens modern man becomes understandable, as does the ever-increasing spate of changes, upheavals and revolutions. And yet the growing sensitivity to that world of dynamism and metamorphosis is itself a factor which increases the restlessness of the world, because it develops like an infectious illness if it is not taken hold of and mastered consciously from within. Restlessness and movement have in this way themselves become an epidemic. They increase year by year—and visibly so on a world scale since 1989—in accordance not with an arithmetic but a geometric progression.

On this turbulent etheric sea with its frequently high-tossed astral waves, it is therefore important to preserve the steadiness and constancy of the ego (the 'I'), as described in the 'little Apocalypse'.† Anthroposophy can be of decisive help in this respect. Modern psychology has been familiar with the phenomenon of empathy since the 1950s. How-

_____
*This Foreword originally appeared in: *Anthroposophische Gesellschaft an der Jahrtausendschwelle*, Dornach 1994.
† Luke 21:25–36.

ever, empathy is but a feeling-like, semi-conscious aspect of the process that was described by Rudolf Steiner as work with the 'after-image'.* Through making oneself conscious of the after-image, one is able to add to every act of perceiving an object with the physical senses — whether it be a stone, a plant, an animal or a human being, or a situation — the etheric reality that belongs to it as an after-image. In this way one is no longer at the mercy of the etheric realm but learns to stand within it. Working with the after-image is not an esoteric path but is, rather, an endeavour to bring the beginnings of a *natural* consciousness of the etheric (which manifest themselves not infrequently in modern man) to full consciousness and, hence, under the rulership of the ego.

At a time when in colleges in the past three or four years it has become apparent that young people are becoming more and more immune or even allergic to any traditional morality, and also to the idealism which inspired the generation some ten years older than themselves, it seemed right and necessary to attempt to deepen an understanding of the after-image; for here we have something which could give young people the courage and confidence to go on living.

---

* Rudolf Steiner, GA 194, *The Archangel Michael*, Anthroposophic Press 1994; the lecture of 30 November 1919 in Dornach. (GA = *Gesamtausgabe*, the collected works of Rudolf Steiner in the original German, published by Rudolf Steiner Verlag, Dornach, Switzerland.)

PART ONE

Baruch Luke Urieli

The Development of the After-Image Faculty in Modern Man and the Sacrifice of Kaspar Hauser

The Phenomenon of Empathy

During the 1950s the American psychologist Carl Rogers noticed the presence of a new faculty in the younger generation for which he used a word originally coined in 1912: *empathy.** In fact, what he was describing is a *process* which has become part of the experience of an ever-increasing number of those born after the end of the Second World War. Empathy arises out of sympathy, love, interest in and compassion for our fellow human being; it enables us to extend our own inner being into that of the other person and directly experience something of his essential nature.

---

* The word *empathy* was first used in 1912 by Theodor Lipps (1851–1914), a German psychologist and philosopher, at a meeting of the Royal Academy of Arts as a translation of the German word *Einfühlung*. The best known part of his teaching is about the phenomenon of *Einfühlung* as defined as projecting oneself into what is seen. One appreciates the other's reaction by projecting oneself into the other. In his two-volume work *Ästhetik* (1903–1906), Lipps makes all artistic appreciation depend upon a similar self-projection into the object. The latter teaching was the subject of his lecture at the British Academy given about two years before his death.

The year 1928 marked the time when this word fully entered English usage, for it was used by Rebecca West in her book *Strange Necessity*, where she writes: 'The active power of empathy which makes the artist, the passive power of empathy which makes the appreciator of art.'

The process which can to some extent be encompassed by the word empathy has four distinct phases:

1. Taking an interest in another person. This quality of inner interest, which demands a kind of 'turning' towards another, is to be found in its most archetypal form in Parzival's words, 'Brother, what ails thee?' Whenever one human being is willing to take an active interest in the existence and destiny of another, to turn towards him, a glimmer of Parzival's question breaks through and enables the person asking the question to extend part of his own being beyond its usual boundaries. It must be emphasised that this act of 'taking an interest in', of 'turning towards', has to be of the utmost purity. Wherever elements of curiosity, adventurism, criticism, self-interest or self-will colour the initial question asked, the quest cannot succeed and harm will be caused both to the one expressing interest and to the one who is approached. We have to learn to look with two differently tuned eyes at the same time—and yet not squint. If we begin to squint, evil arises.

2. The inner perception of the other person. The inner interest described as phase one of the process makes it possible that a part of ourselves can touch or enter—consciously or half-consciously, for a very short while or for several very short periods—the other person and have a glimpse into his essential being.

3. The return. Having perceived our brother or sister in this way, the extended part of our being returns to its home and reunites with the part it left behind. Through this reunion, an echo or resonance is created. Our own inner self resounds.

4. The reading of the resonance. The endeavour to 'read' this resonance leads to images arising in us which ultimately enable us to conceptualise and understand what has been experienced.

It should be pointed out that, whilst the first phase of the process takes place 'in the twinkling of an eye', and the second in short periods of time, the conscious recalling that forms the third phase can take minutes, hours or days and the reading of the resonance anything from seconds and hours to days or even years.

The after-image

The phenomenon recognised by Rogers in the 1950s had already been described by Rudolf Steiner in the second decade of the century and in a much wider context. Whereas Rogers observed the phenomenon in the realm of human encounter and, hence, focused almost exclusively on the second stage of the fourfold process, Rudolf Steiner was aware that the process that has been described is not limited to meetings between human beings. Through turning to the world in this way, the individual can learn to acquire an inner relationship to any phenomenon, any process and any situation. This new faculty which becomes available to mankind was called by Rudolf Steiner the phenomenon of the 'after-image'. It has its foundation in that man is beginning in our time to cross the threshold of the spiritual world in the natural course of his development. This means that our present-day consciousness, which is limited in its perception to the physical world alone, is gradually supplemented by a capacity to perceive the etheric world, the world of living processes.

Rudolf Steiner pays particular attention to phase four of the process and gives the example of the after-image awakened in the eye by coloured objects. In so doing, he makes us aware that every process of visual perception is complemented by a second, complementary process which is, as he stresses, not merely of a physical nature (compare especially the lecture of 30 November 1919 in *The Mission of the Archangel Michael*, also that of 13 January 1924 in *Rosicrucianism and Modern Initiation*, and 27 May 1922, *The Change in the Path to Supersensible Knowledge*: see Appendix). As Steiner says in the lecture of 30 November 1919, the process of seeing crosses with a cosmic process, thereby giving access to the inner quality of all that is encountered. The challenge is to become aware of the second, hidden process.

Anyone who has tried to become aware of the after-image of, say, a coloured piece of material will appreciate how great this challenge is. For he will know that whilst it may be relatively easy to see the exact *form* of the after-image, it will be extremely difficult to be so precise as to its texture and colour; where the more inward quality of the object encountered is about to reveal itself, a mountain of obstacles arises. The experienced observer will also know that the more we want to see these qualities the less we will be able to do so. Here the selflessness of the quest is tested; here the truth of the old saying 'Who wants doesn't get' is confirmed.

In textbooks on colour, the reader is told that to see the after-image he should first concentrate on the central point *within* a ring of colour printed on white and with a cross in the middle, and then transfer his gaze onto a light grey area, again marked in its centre with a cross. The effectiveness of this lies in the fact that in the first stage of the exercise the ring of colour encourages the eye to look in a peripheral way, i.e. the coloured outer ring and its outer surroundings are perceived, while the cross in the middle ensures that the centre is not entirely lost. The eye is thereby taught to be selfless and can fulfil the first phase of the empathetic process, taking in something of the etheric and complementary nature of the coloured ring. In the second stage of the exercise the eye is allowed to return to its ordinary centred direction of sight. The ring is still indicated by the round circumference of the grey area as a help for the memory, and the complementary colour invisible in the first stage can now shine up on the neutral, light-grey surface.

Where a person learns to take an interest in his fellows and the world in such a way that the 'after-image' can arise, he will be able to glimpse something of the inner nature and need not only of another human being but also of a plant in

Then transfer your gaze
to this figure centring it
again on the small cross

Look intensely at the coloured
ring whilst keeping your gaze
firmly centred on the small cross

the garden, an animal in the stable or any difficult situation. He may even be helped in this way to find the solution to a mathematical or mechanical problem, or be led to the place of an object lost or mislaid. New vistas open up if an inner vision can be added to the outer one. In the remarkable book by Agatha Christie *The Mysterious Mr Quin*, the criminal cases are throughout solved with the help of the after-image. This book is of quite a different kind from the rest of Agatha Christie's works, and its twelve stories are well worth reading. It was written at a time when its author had not fully made up her mind whether to become a poet or a writer of crime stories.*

Pure perception and pure thinking

Through the four phases of the after-image process, two different directions of movement can be discerned. First there is the interest, a turning towards, which leads to the perception of the inner state or need of the person/object. Then follows the 'return'; this enables us to resound and, out of the resonance, form mental images and concepts concerning the nature of the person/object. The quality of the mental images or concepts resulting from this process will depend on two factors: the purity of the perceptions initially attained and the purity of the activity of thinking that follows. But this leads to the question: to what extent *can* a human being endeavour to attain to pure perception and pure thinking? It is a question that has been explored in an exemplary way by Hendrik Knobel in two short articles published in *Das Goetheanum* on 2 and 9 May 1982. I shall endeavour to summarise these with some additions of my own.

Hendrik Knobel first of all makes his readers aware that

---

* Agatha Christie, *The Mysterious Mr Quin*, first published in 1930, currently published by Harper Collins; see excerpts on pp.93–103.

under ordinary conditions we can hardly speak about pure perception, since perceptions can only register in our mind when we have already formed those concepts on which they depend. We do not recognise a specific colour, plant, person or object unless we have first formed the necessary concept for it. We miss many details of a holiday journey, a picture gallery, a surprising situation, unless we have prepared the corresponding concepts. The registering of perceptions depends on the concepts available to us and is at the same time coloured by them: 'What an awkward fellow!'; 'The house is just down this road, you cannot miss it.' The well-known fact of a number of observers describing in very different and even contradictory terms an event they have witnessed together is, in the main, not due to weakness in their faculty of perception but to those preconceived concepts with which they meet the situation. Only a small child, who has not yet formed concepts, can live in a world of pure sense-perception. People who are able to remember very early stages of childhood describe a world of coloured spots; form, texture, purpose and meaning become recognisable only in stages. The small child experiences a world of light, colour and movement and, hence, lives in a sphere of pure perception where it 'touches the garments of divinity'. This appears to be unattainable to the adult human being. Hendrik Knobel points out, however, that there once lived a child who was artificially kept in the world of pure perception until his sixteenth year by virtue of being held in solitary confinement in a dark contained space. As a consequence he retained the gift of pure perception upon his re-entry into human society, for a time — that is, until the concepts forced upon him by that society made their impact upon his perceptive faculties, and tainted them. This child was Kaspar Hauser.

The situation concerning pure thinking is of a similar nature. Just as it is practically impossible for the ordinary adult person to register a perception without previously having formed the relevant concept, so is it just as impossible to form a concept of, say, a chair without previously having perceived a number of chairs. Only gradually do we learn to know that, for instance, the brown colour or the wooden material are secondary and replaceable attributes of a chair, while the qualities of supporting the trunk of its occupant and assisting his back into uprightness are essentials. As a result of repeated perception and observation of similar objects or situations, we learn to distil what is essential in them or their inherent meaning and purpose.

Studying this picture can serve to exercise the ability to see the after-image. In the transition from seeing the chalice to seeing the faces, one learns what it means to look in a centrally focused or a peripheral way

Thereby we move from perception to concept, from outer appearance to inner being and meaning.

From the above considerations, it will be obvious that we have to free our perception from the bondage of concepts previously formed if we are to attain to pure perception. We have to move towards a state of *inner childhood*. We have to become young, so young that we can again touch the 'garments of divinity'. On the other hand, in order to attain to pure thinking, we have to remove from our perceptions their outer covering and appearance. This covering must fall away, layer by layer, until we reach the inner nature and meaning of what we have perceived. This demands a growing inner maturity: we have to become *inwardly* old.

The process of empathy, the process of creating the after-image, unites these two elements. In its interest in the world, it approaches pure perception; in its returning to the perceiving self, it wrestles for pure thinking. But it goes a step further still, for the quest is crowned at that moment when, the pure perception and the pure mental image having been reached, the two can fuse for one holy instant. Then, what has been perceived in purity reveals its inner meaning. Man, earth and universe become transparent and radiant. The perception of the idea in its full reality has been reached.

Kaspar Hauser and the after-image

Since the murder of Kaspar Hauser in 1833, hearts and minds have not ceased being shaken by this crime. The tumultuous death of this extraordinary young man, who was shortly afterwards called 'The Child of Europe', has stirred many to the very depths of their existence. And yet just as human life has a number of different levels, so does this crime—and the interest that is centred on it—have many layers.

At its most obvious (and this has caused the widest circle of interest) it was a dynastic crime; and it is this that has gripped the thoughts and sense of justice of the majority of those who have heard or read about Kaspar Hauser. A smaller circle of people have been stirred by Feuerbach's insight that the twelve-year-long solitary confinement of Kaspar Hauser was an attempt to destroy a human soul. A new kind of crime thereby became visible for those who could recognise it. This has been an inspiration to many to become healers of human beings in need of soul-care. On the other hand, since 1933, the centenary of Kaspar Hauser's death, it has also led others to join those who wish to perfect the crime which succeeded only in part.

A still smaller circle of people have been able to discern a third level. When Feuerbach realised that the twelve-year imprisonment was a crime against a human soul, he was puzzled as to why such a method should have been preferred to outright murder. Insights obtained from Rudolf Steiner suggest that when the life of someone as out of the ordinary as Kaspar Hauser is forcibly cut short a new, influential incarnation can be expected very soon after — an incarnation that will fulfil the great cultural and political tasks destined for the former life. Thus the purpose of the long period of imprisonment, in which Kaspar's mental development was arrested by solitary confinement, was to tear his personal destiny out of the web of destiny of his contemporaries, making him into a Rip van Winkle who had lost the connection with his times. That seamless garment of destiny which every human being weaves with the help of the divine Hierarchies and other disembodied souls before returning to earth — that garment had been torn. A new kind of crime, a crime against *destiny* — that is, a crime against both human and divine beings — had been committed, with the result that Kaspar Hauser became unable to fulfil his predestined mission, which was to prepare — in Central Europe — the cultural, political and economic basis for the new Age of Light.* It can therefore appear that the Powers of Darkness were successful in preventing Kaspar Hauser's mission from being fulfilled. However, if we follow the story of Kaspar's life closely, it becomes evident that, while failing in his outer mission, he developed a new, inner faculty which represented an indestructible replacement of what he would otherwise have been able to achieve.

For the first three years of his life, Kaspar was placed in a somewhat normal human environment, since it was known to the perpetrators of this crime against destiny that a child under three who is denied human contact will invariably fade away and die—a fact verified experimentally by Frederick II (1194–1250), German Emperor and King of Sicily. It was no doubt assumed by those who masterminded the crime that the prolonged solitary confinement which followed would break him mentally and reduce him to a demented human being. The letters given to him at the time of his appearance in Nuremberg confirm this. However, neither the physical nor the human deprivation of Kaspar Hauser's imprisonment managed to overpower him. On the contrary, his outer senses became so keen that he was able to see in near darkness and could smell, taste, touch and hear things imperceptible to other human beings. Descriptions of his extraordinary sensitivity, especially during the Nuremberg period, bear ample witness to this. So in fact, Kaspar Hauser's imprisonment brought about a result totally unforeseen and unwanted by his captors, namely, the attainment of a capacity for pure sense-perception untainted by any conceptual influence or by an education imparted through concepts.

His enemies had, therefore, to make every possible effort

---

* Cf. Rudolf Steiner, GA 118; especially the lecture of 25 January 1910, 'The Event of Christ's Appearance in the Etheric World', published in *The Reappearance of Christ in the Etheric*, Anthroposophic Press 1983. The year 1899 was both the end of the Kali Yuga and the beginning of the Age of Light.

to transfer him to an environment where conceptual influence would taint or annihilate these extraordinary gifts. His guardianship was transferred from Tucher to Stanhope and his education from Daumer to Meyer. However, again something unforeseen occurred. The extreme suffering imposed upon Kaspar Hauser by his solitary confinement had not caused inner hardening or defiance but, rather, a boundless intensification of his concern and love for the weakness, failure or pain of others. While he certainly remained afraid of the man who kept him in prison, he bore him no hatred; on the contrary, he felt a deep compassion for him, for this man lived in constant fear of his crime being discovered. And this extreme inner sensitivity towards (indeed *empathy* with) his surroundings, which had developed during the twelve years of his imprisonment, protected him later on against the forming of superficial, abstract or inhumane concepts.

Then about one and a half years after his appearance, there was an attempt on his life which, however, misfired. The continuous threat under which he lived following this attack, together with his meeting with true Christianity in Daumer, Tucher, Feuerbach and especially Pastor Fuhrmann, who prepared him for his confirmation, served only to enhance his sensitivity—to the extent that, in spite of all the opposing circumstances, he was able to form mental images and concepts of extraordinary purity. And so a perceptive faculty of high purity was united with the development of a thinking which was tainted only to a very small degree. This resulted in life becoming ever more transparent to Kaspar himself; and so it was that something of the essential truth of his destiny began to filter through to him and, consequently, to others. Without doubt, this led to the decision that Kaspar Hauser must be killed.

Kaspar Hauser died on 17 December 1833, after he had forgiven his murderer, amid the accusations and lies of a miserable schoolmaster seeking to clear his own name by besmirching the character of his charge. Yet evil had *not* triumphed; for by the time of his death, a new trail had been 'blazed' for mankind. A perceptivity of the highest innocence had been united with a power of thinking purified by the deepest suffering, enabling light to enter the earthly gloom and make it transparent and radiant. With the appearance of this new gift on the earth, mankind was now equipped for that onslaught by the Powers of Darkness which began to build up a hundred years later and which has increased in force ever since. The gift of empathy, the capacity to form after-images which penetrate earth existence and unveil its inner meaning, found its way to earth through the sacrificial deed of Kaspar Hauser. In this way, a tool has been given to humanity by means of which it can free itself from the encapsulation intended by the Dark Powers.

The Atlantean betrayal and its redemption

When Rudolf Steiner was first asked about Kaspar Hauser, he remarked that he was a misplaced Atlantean!* This can

---

* 'Some years ago Dr Steiner had said to my mother that Kaspar Hauser was a "straggler from Atlantis". My mother often told this story when we went to Daumer's house.' (Rudolf Rissmann, 'Rudolf Steiner Anfang des Jahrhunderts', in: *Erinnerungen an Rudolf Steiner*, Stuttgart 1979, p.29.)

Rudolf Steiner, 'according to a well-authenticated report, referred to Kaspar Hauser as a *straggler from Atlantis*. This happened around 1905/6 in a conversation with someone from Nuremberg who had asked Rudolf Steiner about Kaspar Hauser and whose own parents had been close friends of Prof. Daumer's. Whatever one may discern from this observation, it must at any rate have been the case that Kaspar Hauser manifested traits that were characteristic of the Atlanteans. This is also in keeping with the strength of his memory' (Karl Heyer, *Kaspar Hauser und das Schicksal Mitteleuropas*, Kressborn 1958, p.21). Both quoted in Peter Tradowsky, *Kaspar Hauser: The Struggle for the Spirit. A contribution towards an understanding of the nineteenth and twentieth centuries* (Temple Lodge 1997).

lead to the observation that the sensory faculties of soul which he manifested on his appearance in Nuremberg on Whit Monday 1828 were very similar to the faculties of an Atlantean, and to the conclusion that Kaspar Hauser's mission in our time was related to tasks unfulfilled by mankind during the Atlantean period. Let us look at these two aspects in more detail.

It was in the second half of the Lemurian period* that human beings began to stand back from the world around them. Up to then they had lived passively in a sea of impressions, taking them in as long as they lasted but unable to ward them off, filter them, grasp them or hold them as memory. The Lemurian Mysteries introduced a training in which men had to undergo trials against threatening nature-forces while women watched. The men had to develop an active will to survive (a last remnant of this can be found in the puberty rites of, for instance, some African tribes) while the women developed their powers of imagination through their experiences (enabling them to become leaders and seers, guides of the people; early societies in the history of humanity were led by women). For both, it was the means of taking hold of their impressions and perceptions.

As long as men or women were unable to take hold of their sensory impressions, they were also unable to describe the world or influence it through language. They were merely able to make sounds of joy or pain, just as an animal does when overwhelmed by an instinctive emotion. Only when they acquired a conscious response to their perceptions could the first rudiments of speech develop. We can therefore imagine man in the early Atlantean period as being equipped with a very keen and pure perceptive

---

*Regarding the Lemurian period, see Rudolf Steiner, *Occult Science*, Rudolf Steiner Press 1979, GA 13, and *Cosmic Memory*, Rudolf Steiner Publications 1971, GA 11, the chapter entitled 'The Lemurian Race'.

faculty, with the first rudiments of speech and a memory able to form images as keen as the perceptions it recalled (if only for a very short period of time, after which the impressions had to be recalled again by outer means; this was the purpose of the standing stones and cairns of that time).

We must realise, however, that speech and language in those early days had a different quality from that which they have today. Since language grew out of very pure perception, its imagery was so close to life that it could influence and even rule it. To 'spell a name' meant, in those primeval times, that a spell would be put on the owner of that name, be it man, animal or plant. Through speech that was the creative inner transformation of the power of life, man became a ruler of life.

Progressively, during the second and third periods of the Atlantean age, man learned to interiorise his memory through rhythmical repetition. Before this time he needed the help of outward signs such as cairns, notches, runes or knots, just as we still avail ourselves of such methods today when we can no longer rely on our memory. This development from a 'local memory', still wholly bound to external sense-perceptions, to a memory dependent on rhythmical repetition and finally to an intellectual memory is one through which every human being has to pass from childhood to adulthood. With the help of the growing continuity of memory, man was able to build up ever wider social relationships. Previous deeds and achievements began to be a part of life. Traditions, customs, laws began to develop, a tribal commonwealth could be formed. But along with all this came the temptation to gain power for one's own ends.

At first, the power over life given to Atlantean man through speech had been used only as a sacred instrument, and in accordance with the aims of those who were the true guides of humanity. But gradually the results of the Fall of

Man in Lemuria* began to show. The fourth Atlantean period was dominated by a culture that attempted to use the sun power for its own, selfish ends. Remains of that dark culture still exist today in Central Asia, among the Shamans of Turania. One of their symbols is the sun-wheel in the form of a swastika—a symbol which achieved worldwide notoriety in 1933. To combat the misuse of the life-forces, the leaders of the Mysteries began to develop *thinking* in man; for concepts are none other than dead, fossilised life-forces. Man, removed from his closeness to life, lost his power over it. But instead, a seed was sown inside him which was to lead later, in the post-Atlantean age, to a conscious and independent mastery of the world—even though it led at first to the gradual destruction of the Atlantean culture.

Against the above background, Kaspar Hauser, as he appeared in the summer of 1828, can indeed be seen as a stray Atlantean: the purity and sensitivity of his sense-perceptions; the rudimentary nature of his speech; his possession of a keen memory, though one which was at first completely bound to particular places and rhythms and only gradually became able to recall earlier events from within; his closeness to animals and his mastery over them; his affinity to everything in life that is pure and true—all these gifts reveal him as a true Atlantean. Yet he was an Atlantean not by nature but due to a crime against the human soul, a crime that wished to imprison him in a previous state of human existence in order to incapacitate his mind. When these machinations failed, there was the attempt to lead him on a path of destruction (as happened on a large scale in Atlantis). Stanhope tried to induce him to use his special gifts for exploiting his fellow human beings and so misuse his powers. And indeed, Kaspar did begin to flatter and be untruthful here and there. But this was

---

*See Rudolf Steiner, *Cosmic Memory*, 'Our Atlantean Ancestors'.

incompletely successful; and he was therefore brought to Meyer, whose task it was to taint and deaden the pure life-forces active within him with a dry, intellectual education.

But just at this moment something took place in the life of Kaspar Hauser which those powers opposed to the Sun Mysteries could neither foresee nor understand. From one who had not previously incarnated in Christian times and who was held back by occult machinations at an Atlantean stage of development, with his confirmation and the preparation for it there gushed forth a fountain of true Christianity much stronger than any teacher could give. This can only be explained to one who has learned through Rudolf Steiner that the Mystery of Golgotha was preceded by three pre-earthly deeds of Christ, two of which took place during the Atlantean age.* There was no doubt an intimate connection between the individuality of Kaspar Hauser and that angelic being who was then the bearer of the Christ.†

When it became clear that Kaspar Hauser had completely broken out of his occult fetters, he was killed. But the killers were too late! A way had been opened for mankind whereby its attaining of an expanded consciousness represented an opportunity to use these new powers in freedom and in a Christian way.

To grasp the immense significance of this, we have to make ourselves aware of the fact that it was in the middle of the Atlantean period, that is, right in the middle of our evolution, that the Christ should have united Himself with the earth. Then the whole of mankind, under His guidance, would have become the co-ordinators of a world of pure life-forces. But as a result of the Fall during the Lemurian age, selfishness crept in. The Atlantean Sun Mysteries were betrayed and the dark Turanian epoch replaced the in-

---

* See Rudolf Steiner, *Pre-Earthly Deeds of Christ*, Steiner Book Centre 1976, 7 March 1914 (GA 152).

† See Peter Tradowsky, op. cit., p.255 and the last paragraph of p.282.

tended Christ Event. Man lost access to that world of the life-forces in which he had lived and was forced to incarnate much too deeply into physical existence. The maya existence of the post-Atlantean age arose as a result of man's falling prey to the temptation of Lucifer. Man, hoping to become like God, as Lucifer had promised him in Lemuria, became the opposite and sank earthwards.

With the actual Christ Event, the Mystery of Golgotha, set in a much later time, the scales have been tipped for a mankind in decline. Something new in earth existence begins to develop, something of the sun-filled cosmic nature of the earth manifests itself once again. Those human beings who can find a free and independent relationship to Christ can unite with this impulse and can regain — in a free and conscious way — access to that sphere in which they had previously been meant to live as collaborators with the Hierarchies in the Atlantean age. The decisive point in this development comes in the twentieth century, when mankind is starting to 'cross the threshold', as Rudolf Steiner expressed it. To our normal *centred* consciousness is gradually being added an *expanded* consciousness — one that was natural in Atlantis and is still natural in a state of dream or sleep, but one that would return man to the passive state of a rudderless boat on an open sea were he unable to activate an *inner* rudder and motor.

It is therefore no wonder that people today are overwhelmed by the influences coming to meet them and swept away by powerful spiritual currents. A vast panorama, extending from drugs and the obsession with sex to membership of the most varied spiritual movements promising inner experiences or 'liberation', has opened up before us as evidence of our beginning to 'float' in a disorientated way. Atlantis is on the point of returning, and we of being swamped by our past. Forces of an inhuman nature rise in waves and attempt to drag mankind into the abyss of loss of independence and destruction. Only his freest and purest core, that divine spark of the Christ-endowed man within man or, as St Paul said, of 'Not I, but the Christ in me' can be rudder and motor in his storm-tossed existence.

Kaspar Hauser was the first human being in modern times to be flung back into Atlantean waters. Yet out of his intimate connection with the Christian Mysteries he was able to forge the new ability of creating the 'after-image' — the ability to 'turn towards' in pure perception, and then to 're-turn' to pure mental image — suffusing the darkness of earth existence with radiant light. That is Kaspar Hauser's victory.

The archetype of the after-image

In the seventh chapter of the Gospel of St Luke it is related how a woman washed the feet of Christ with her tears, dried them with her hair and then anointed them with precious ointment, much to the disdain of the self-righteous Pharisee hosting the Christ who said to himself, 'If this man were a prophet, he would know who and what sort of woman this is who is touching him, for she is a sinner.' Christ, who had perceived the Pharisee's thought, answered His host by reminding him that *he* had not even offered Him water with which to wash His feet; neither had he welcomed Him with a kiss, while the woman had not ceased to kiss His feet; and he had not anointed His head with oil, as was customary with well-favoured guests (compare Psalm 23:5), whereas she had anointed it with precious ointment. Therefore, as He points out to His host, her sins, which were many, are forgiven, for she 'loved much'.*

This woman is Mary Magdalene. In the presence of Christ, her misguided powers of love regain balance and

---

* Luke 7:47.

direction and eventually lead both her sister, Martha, and her brother, Lazarus, to Him. Later, Mary repeats her first deed of love: six days before the Crucifixion, she anoints the feet of Jesus Christ and four days later, His head, thus preparing Him for death.* On Easter morning Mary is the first to go to the tomb and discover that the stone has been rolled away. She calls Peter and her brother and runs back with them to the tomb. When the two men have left again in amazement and consternation, she remains, weeping. Then she stoops down to look into the tomb where, instead of the empty space which the two men had seen, she sees two angels. One sits at the place where Christ's head had lain — the head which she had anointed — and the other where had lain the feet she had anointed. When the angels ask her why she is weeping she turns and sees Jesus, yet without recognising Him, thinking Him to be the gardener. Then He also asks her why she is weeping and calls her by name. She turns once more and recognises the One who had trans-formed her life and been her guide. She perceives the Risen One.†

These events show in archetype what empathy and after-image are and how they work. Love and compassion in their pure form are together the new power of will which is able to build the hierarchic space in which alone an event like the above can take place. They give us the motivation and strength to reach out towards the 'garment of divinity'. In this space we can inwardly turn towards those worlds of experience which would otherwise escape our ordinary vision, even though we cannot as yet conceptualise and understand them, make them meaningful. For that further step to happen we must *turn* once more, we must *re-turn* to that space which is the home of our 'I am', the space where our name resounds. There the event we have experienced

---

* John 12:1–8 and Mark 14:1–9.
† John 20:1–16.

can reverberate within us and thus begin to reveal its true significance and meaning. Then our confusion, suffering and sorrow can become joy.

The great power of love, redirected and healed by the Christ and His sacrifice, which shines in Mary Magdalene, becomes in Kaspar Hauser the individual, conscious path which suffering and sacrifice can blaze through the darkness. In the temptations and trials, the suffering, sacrifice and victory of Mary Magdalene, 'who loved much', the present generation can recognise themselves and find their own way forward.

Hans Müller-Wiedemann

Cultivating the Social Ethic

I

The intention of the essay that follows is to characterise the creative processes in which the human individual can engage in the course of building up social relationships. The essay is based on experiences relating to this theme together with the fruits of Rudolf Steiner's spiritual-scientific research on social renewal, in particular his lectures of 30 November 1919* and of 10 November of the same year.†

Even as he was giving lectures on the forming of new social and political structures, Rudolf Steiner was aware that the 'social principle' or 'social impulse' through which people in modern times have expressed their need for new forms of social life after the upheavals of the First World War represented above all a challenge to the will of the individual. This individual will can consciously free itself in a twofold way from its natural bondage to the bodily nature with which it remains entwined if not cultivated in this fashion. The experiences that derive from this process become fruitful for one's relationship with another person and for perceiving him socially. For people today, such an exercise can be stimulated by the pain that one may experience because of the entrenched nature of old ways of thinking and living; and the need for renewal and reform is

---

* Rudolf Steiner, *The Mission of the Archangel Michael*, Anthroposophic Press 1980 (GA 194).
† Rudolf Steiner, 'Der Geist als Führer durch die Sinnes- und in die übersinnliche Welt', contained in the volume entitled *Die Befreiung des Menschenwesens als Grundlage für eine soziale Neuentfaltung* (GA 329). See translation of excerpt on page 65.

felt whenever the growing alienation between one person and another, and the decline of old social structures associated with it, thrusts itself into one's daily awareness. Rudolf Steiner's impulse to make his spiritual-scientific research in the form of an 'anthroposophy' fruitful for social life arose out of his experience of this situation of humanity, which has become so dramatically evident in our present century. In this new way in which the individual may cultivate inclining his will towards his fellow human being, there lies the seed of a new social ethic and — as a method — a 'social art'.

The cognitive method inherent in such a training, to which Baruch Urieli has drawn attention in his essay, is closely connected with the phenomenon of the after-images of sensory manifestations, on the one hand, and, on the other, with the freeing of the will from its desire-nature, in order that the will residing in the other person may be perceived and awakened to life in one's own soul. In his essay, Urieli has described these two processes whereby a capacity for social knowledge and perception may be forged anew in a soul-spiritual way, referring to them by means of the concept of 'empathy' widely used by the American psychologist Carl Rogers.

In the case of social life it needs to be borne in mind that the after-image of sensory perceptions can manifest itself only if — that is, it appears under the condition that — the customary 'processing' of visible phenomena as is familiar from the scientific method of forming mental pictures, recalling them and developing concepts, is held back. Moreover, there is a need for a 'pure' and exact perception of visible phenomena, so that the sense-world is able to manifest itself as *it itself* wants. Only through these two strict conditions can the circumstances be created for a new soul-spiritual perceptual phenomenon in the form of the rapidly fading after-image, the seed of imaginations. We may recall that the classical cognitive method of natural science, when employed in 'sociology', has played a disastrous role in both theory and practice right into present times; its method is to gain power over the objects of knowledge within its frame of reference with the intention of mastering them and, hence, accepts no limits to its sovereignty. In his dispute extending over many years with classical science, Goethe sensed this relationship which has become so obvious today; and at the end of his life he prophetically foresaw this danger. He realised that the perceiving, observing and cognising human being has to be constantly examining his inner attitude and changing it in accordance with the objects of his cognition if, rather than 'screw down' the world of appearances, he is to enable it to find itself again in the soul of the one who is observing it, that is, to know itself. The after-image is a first tentative step on this path of knowledge. Out of this seedlike substance, imaginations eventually begin to arise in the mind's eye. Such answers of the soul, whose significance can dawn upon us in the context of social life, are like seeds springing from an ancient soil. According to Steiner, the memory-pictures that want to appear must be held back. The will-imbued formative forces that are unconsciously at work in the ordinary way that memories are evoked are made available for perception; the will turns from imprisoning itself in the past through the evoking of memories to creating the after-image, whose characteristics are tenderness and lack of bondage to the earth.

If the 'pure' inner attitude to phenomena forged by the will is maintained, the after-image can take on a more 'densified' quality. The after-images that have been engendered by the etheric life-forces come to be permeated by living thinking. In this way, objects of contemplation—growing, as it were, out of a will that has 'been taken in hand' (the soul-attitude of loving attention)—arise in the mind's eye, the living idea arises with the character of supersensible perception (like Goethe's archetypal plant) and, finally,

Imagination in the spiritual-scientific sense is born.

This 'living thinking' at the same time demonstrates its character, in that it does not destroy the etheric nature of the after-image process and — for the person who follows this process through — brings the extreme state of becoming free from the bodily organisation of the brain to a certain degree of consciousness. Rudolf Steiner himself referred in various ways to the transition from the creation of after-images to Imagination, as for example when — in connection with perceiving the visible human form — he draws attention to the fact that something remains over from the after-image which no longer has to do with the organ of seeing but is an experience of the etheric body.* He explains that once one has arrived at a proper picture of the visible human form it is possible to *fix* the structure resounding in the etheric body into an imagination, which one may have before one supersensibly in the etheric realm. It should be borne in mind that the process whereby an imagination arises cannot be remembered in the ordinary sense. As with the building up of conscience, it has to be created ever anew. Rudolf Steiner expresses it as follows: 'If we use our power of memory not in order to remember as such but so that the ideas and mental pictures which are otherwise kept alive only through the power of memory may be allowed to remain consciously present in our mind, we strengthen something in our mind through which we may — when the necessary time for this has arrived — come to know of a quite different kind of awakening from that which we experience every morning.'† Steiner's words about the 'necessary time' make it clear that the act of imagining has to do with a moment of 'presence of mind'‡ or calling

---

* Rudolf Steiner, *Man in the Light of Occultism, Theosophy and Philosophy*, Rudolf Steiner Press 1964: the lecture of 10 June 1912 (GA 137).

† See second note on p.24.

‡ The German word for 'presence of mind', *Geistesgegenwart*, means liaterally 'the spirit-present'. — Tr.

[something] to mind, which 'resurrects' the forces of the past (the physical factors of mental picturing, memory and the capacity to form concepts) in such a way that they are now freed for the future from factors depending upon the body in the supersensible faculty of Imagination. Goethe had a sense for this future potential in his study of the archetypal plant; it was for him a 'created thing', the contemplation of which in the 'eye of the soul' made one aware of the potential inherent in sense-perceptible reality, the endless invention of new plant forms from the creative ground of the archetypal plant. Here—to express the gist of Goethe's idea—something historically new was initiated that was not understood by classical science: the beginning of a method of cognition which was fully developed later by Rudolf Steiner and which he endeavoured to make increasingly fruitful expressly for social life. In the lecture of 30 November referred to earlier, he introduces a characterisation of the Michael age through the example of the after-image and continues these remarks by speaking about the threefold social organism as an impulse of the Michael thought as conceived by man. It is there that the answer is given to the question of the objective reality of both after-image and imagination.

Where do imaginations live? The weight of the question in the context of history can in social life today be experienced as a necessity. It finds an answer in the working of the spirit-being of Michael in the nineteenth century, through which a new possibility was created for man to collaborate in the further evolution of the Earth and of humanity. Through the working of Michael in the spiritual world the spirit-sphere of the cosmos was as it were clarified and 'purified', so that it became receptive to the spiritual impulses proceeding from man. Since the last third of the nineteenth century, Michael has been able to expect these impulses. This Michael sphere bordering on the earthly world in the cosmic ether is the spiritual place where imaginations live as objective spiritual realities when they are created by human beings. It is Michael's concern that man should become his collaborator in forming world events, with all the consequences that result for his historical conscience and above all for the shaping of the social life of humanity in accordance with spiritual ideals.

Michael waits for human beings on the threshold of the etheric world bordering upon the physical world. Through his deed in the first half of the nineteenth century of purifying the heavens and banishing the powers of darkness to the earth, he has created that spiritual domain where — since the last third of the past century — human deeds become objective supersensible realities beyond the threshold. It is there where the Christ works together with Michael and enables the imaginations created by human beings on earth as a first stage of supersensible knowledge to become reality. Because of this they cease to be mere subjective phenomena but become objectively inscribed into world evolution.*

Wherever in a community of human beings a real effort is made to find the imaginative picture of the other person, we make the beings of the spiritual world inclined to turn towards us, following the gesture of Michael as it points towards man. In every thought that we dedicate to the other person, a gentle imaginative power can live which works in such a way as to foster relationships, or it may be the antisocial, divisively working shadow of mere ideas and fixed memory-pictures. From the living material of social imaginations the mantle of a society is woven. It can be perceived today wherever people live together as an objective supersensible fact, as a climate in which souls can breathe the air of the spirit. A new attentiveness is able to

---

* Rudolf Steiner, *Anthroposophical Leading Thoughts*, Rudolf Steiner Press 1985 (GA 26), pp.183–85., and *The Fall of the Spirits of Darkness*, Rudolf Steiner Press 1993 (GA 177), lecture 9.

perceive the light or darkness of this supersensible weaving between human beings. It manifests itself in conferences as much as it does in the everyday encounters of life. One becomes a socially responsible colleague through the individual striving for this form-creating experience. No outward organisational form of life can replace the ever to be renewed impulse in the soul to bring the light of Imagination to the will. In the image of the dawn, with which the rising sun proclaims itself anew on the horizon, we may gain an impression of the soul in its capacity to paint imaginations on the canvas of the cosmic ether.

II

We shall now turn to the other aspect, the training of the will, which — alongside the creating of after-images and the faculty of Imagination — represents the other side of the concept of empathy in the sense intended by Rogers. These two aspects do not stand in a physically conditioned causal relationship to one another. The experience of their mutual affinity only arises beyond the threshold between the sense-world and the world of the supersensible. The forces of will-transformations — in the various ways in which they arise within the soul — manifest themselves in their totality and interrelatedness only if (through practice) they come into view and are illuminated supersensibly. In this way the stages, relationships or phases which Urieli has described are also revealed, and ultimately the coming together of the two elements in question: turning to the being of the other in inner perception, and the after-image resonance of the meeting and the understanding of it.

The social realities that can stimulate the cultivating of the second — will — exercise have in our century manifested themselves in a radical way through solitude and estrangement between people, and through the loss of

blood-relationships (which have been becoming increasingly weak since the fifteenth century) and social relationships based upon tradition. This means that at the high-
point of the natural process of individuation, and the freedom associated with it, modern man at the same time loses
the protective mantle of the old social fabric. This historical
process comes to its most characteristic focus in the relation
between one person and another. The existentialist movement in this century has—especially through the work of
Sartre—illuminated the situation philosophically and also
dramatically. In both smaller (family) and larger social
contexts, it is now sharply and painfully in our present
consciousness. The gravity of the situation is as great as the
difficulty appears to be to bring about any change or
transformation. It is a case of freeing the will, bound as it is
to the body, that is, to the digestive system, through which
the individual normally acts from within outwards, from
those body-bound processes and—in the encounter with
the other human being—opening up the thus liberated will
to this person, that is, living into the will of the other. A
new, no longer organically blood-bound form of encounter
between human beings needs to be established, where
something passes from the will-nature of the one person to
the will-nature of the other. The condition of this way of
meeting is the freeing of the will that is being directed
towards another person from the desire-nature of the soul,
which is generally active in the will. Only in this renunciation can the purity of the perception of the inner being of
the other emerge for a few moments. What can in such a
case be communicated as a revelation of the will of the other
to one's own soul-life has no sharp contours. It appears
similarly to a dream in sleep. In his description of the soul-
attitude that lies at the foundation of such an inclining of a
will towards another person that has been freed from its
desire-nature, Rudolf Steiner characterises this quality of
loving attention as the same which the individual has to

bring forth when his will learns to direct itself not towards
what is external to that other person but towards his own
inherent biographical impulses of development.* He then
himself begins to take his development in hand in this act of
perceiving, that is, in directing his externally oriented will
inwards. His own biographical powers of intuition, the
moral sources of his development, begin to make themselves dimly felt. They flow to him out of the spiritual world
beyond the threshold when he directs his will inwards and
creates a desire-free space within his soul. Whereas the will
otherwise always works from within outwards, in the same
way that desires are ruled by outer reality, so can it—by
contrast—be directed inwards. In that we practise self-
discipline through our will, in that we try to make ourselves
better and better in one way or another, we are drawing
upon that power of will which is free of desire. Only
through cultivating this faculty can the process of inclining
one's will towards another person be made lastingly possible, and it can also prepare for it. In the act of inclining the
desire-free will towards the other we introduce its intuitional quality into our own impulse of development. Our
own ego-nature touches and receives that of the other
differently from a blood-relationship established in this life.
The inner nature of the other, which goes through repeated
earthly lives, becomes perceivable for a moment, shows its
spiritual affinity with me, wafts like a supersensible breath
of magic into social life. We begin to discover the community of ego-beings in a new dimension of 'brotherly
love'.

'But in so far as we enter into the other person in this way,
it is as though everything that pulsates in us, that lives
within us as will, were to receive the will of the other. We
inwardly step right over to the other person. It is as though
we leave our body and enter into the body of the other. If

*See second note on p.24.

this feeling increasingly takes the upper hand, if it spreads out lovingly to others as what I should like to call modern brotherly love, a real life-experience is engendered from this sharing in the will, in the entire soul-life of the other person.'* In that the supersensible world of the spirit shines in through this act of empathy, a communion is brought about in the etheric world whereby the Christ Himself weaves the cosmic intentions in human egos together in a body-free way for a future community of all human beings. Is it perhaps a presentiment of this which calls young people together in present-day social life to form communities?

The attitude that has been described in this section can become the gateway for the blossoming of a free cultural life in certain existing social work-situations, in therapeutic meetings and conferences; and indeed, it is a condition for this. Through the acts of this inclining of the will towards the other person participating in a conference, a free space is created in which the will-impulse of the other—his intuitional qualities—can come to life and are also welcomed as an enrichment to processes of social judgement or development. Experience shows that the individual must and can make ever-renewed commitments to this attitude, in so far as he has learnt to recognise the other in his true spiritual ego-nature as an eternal being who wants and is able to reveal himself in the present in a social space that has been made free. It will not escape the attentive observer of social formative processes that such an attitude and its fruits in individual human beings calls at the same time for an imaginative picturing faculty *of a spiritually living kind* such as is not to be found in the world of the senses. If the cultivation of the will as described in this section is taken hold of by the power of memory summoned from the realm of the unconscious, 'the individual will then know himself

---

* Ibid.

inwardly as a spirit, he will know that he has inwardly taken hold of the spirit in a purely spiritual way ... that he has not achieved this through the organs of the body. He will know about spiritual activity in the spirit, he will know what it means to say that soul and spirit are independent of the body.'* The individual will then awaken from his customary body-bound or body-supported (B. Hardorp) mental picturing, feeling and will, giving rise to another person who is able to work towards the fashioning of social life in accordance with spiritual laws. This person will initially appear in social contexts as delicate and vulnerable, and a training in *attentiveness* in social life is necessary in order to discover him alongside his ordinary self and ultimately create life-circumstances which further his development. On this path of training, a form of that quality of letting the other come into his own—which Rudolf Steiner, in its highest aspect, called interpretation—can develop in one's own soul. This cannot be entered into here. Heten Wilkens has recently referred to the significance of the development of this social art between people in the context of history for the present and future of the social life of our civilisation.†

III

In this concluding section, two additional aspects will be touched upon which amplify what has been said so far.

Firstly, mention must be made of one of the numerous exercises which Rudolf Steiner gave for the renewal of social life as a means of illuminating and widening one's consciousness.‡ He describes it as 'pertaining to general

---

* Ibid.
† Heten Wilkens, *Das Wiedergefundene Wort: Zur Mysterienkultur der Gegenwart*, Stuttgart 1990, pp.205–30.
‡ Rudolf Steiner, *Social and Anti-Social Forces in the Human Being*, Mercury Press 1982 (GA 186).

education', so as to underline its general validity and biographical applicability. One learns through a kind of review
of one's life to get away from seeing oneself as the centre of
the experience of one's past. The aim of the exercise is to
objectify oneself, to extricate one's own ego from the
experiences of the past. Through this we learn to regard our
biographical past in such a way that the individuals who
have had an affect on us and with whom we have had a
connection appear before our mind's eye so clearly that we
ourselves 'can seem as though we are the products of these
people'. Rudolf Steiner continues his characterisation of this
exercise by saying that 'we thereby gradually also acquire
an imaginative relationship to those individuals whom we
meet in the present'. The double aspect already referred to
of the exercises relating to developing the will is also in
evidence here; in this process of objectifying, the will is
released from the experiences concerning one's own self
and becomes free to turn towards the other person, who in a
second step now — in place of the body-bound will-activity
of the memory-picture — stands in the realm of perceptions
before the soul as an imagination. Steiner draws attention to
the fact that this activity of making a picture of the other
present within oneself without hate or love, letting the other
person be resurrected in oneself, is a quality which '. . . with
every week in human evolution is — I would say — more or
less disappearing, it is something which people are gradually completely losing'. Through the exercise envisaged
here, a sense is released from our soul. This new sense
which is fashioned by man himself can — if we confront
human beings in the present 'face to face' — truly enable
presence of mind* to enter social life.

A second aspect of the study of human biographical
development leads us to consider the phenomena in child
development from which the rudiments of what later arises

---

*See third note on p.27.

as the free power of Imagination and the free inclining of the will to the other can be discerned, as yet still in a body-bound form. The liberating of both these new faculties in the Michael age and the description which Rudolf Steiner has given our civilisation of this new capacity have their precursors in early childhood; in these precursors, bound as they are to both organs and body, the power of Imagination is at work, as is the power which extends to the will of the other person in empathy. I am speaking of the little child's faculty of *imitation*, which is bestowed upon the newly born child with the physical birth of the human body. In the first half of this century, the American child psychologist Erik Erikson drew attention to a soul-power of the newly born child which perfectly characterises earliest childhood. He referred to it by means of the concept of *a sense of basic trust*, a soul quality with which the child addresses the sense-world and the other people in its environment. By a sense of basic trust he meant that primal, innocent and uncondi-tional childlike reaching out in which the magic of early childhood lights up before us and at the same time alarms and concerns us in its vulnerability. In this will-activity of the senses, however, the power of Imagination also sleeps in the early years of childhood as a supersensible reality. It becomes a formative power within the body that extends right into the child's movements, even into the forming of the organs of the physical body.

As what has been perceived in the human environment through empathy is reproduced in the body, the power of Imagination manifests itself—in a body-bound way—as imitation. The spiritual-scientific study of man can show how around the seventh year the imagination begins to become free from the working of the organs in the body as the bodily formative processes are transformed into the picturing soul-quality of the schoolchild's memory. In this process that develops in the second seven-year period of life, the capacity to imitate simultaneously dwindles. The personal experience of memory-pictures temporarily drowns the original empathetic power of the sense of basic trust. The child internalises itself. A critical distancing with regard to the world now becomes the characteristic stance of the child's soul-nature. The departure from early childhood is expressed in developmental terms as inner experience. As one becomes older, the faculty of imagination is exerted in the building up of memory.* Only in a third step of evolution, significantly with the onset of puberty in the third seven-year period, do the demands of social life begin in a small way to thrust the young person into that situation whereby the claims of a burgeoning freedom are wrested from what is given naturally through the body. This happens at that point of development when the young person is confronted with the social circumstances of his incarnation, and the question of freedom — and the associated responsibility for development — gives rise to new steps in development amidst outer storms; the question of the possibilities inherent in reaching beyond blood-relationships and learning to perceive the inner being of the other person, together with the second metamorphosis of the imagination into a 'sense' freed from organic life, becomes ever more pressing. With the gaining of the faculties associated with this — which have been the subject of the foregoing — life with other people can begin to become transparent for the young person today through the liberating metamorphosis from bondage to the body.†

The purpose of these developmental considerations is to draw attention to the point in our biography when we as it were *in statu nascendi* experience the emerging of the sense for social relationships out of the state of being bound to the body. In a remarkable work bearing the subtitle *Das soziale*

---

* Hans Müller-Wiedemann, *Mitte der Kindheit*, Stuttgart 1993, pp.138–58.
† See second note on p.24, and also the lecture of 6 November 1919 from the same (untranslated) volume.

Leben als Entwicklungsfeld des Menschen ('Social Life as a Field of Human Development'), Benedictus Hardorp has in an exemplary way traced this theme which can be discerned on the individual level in the general context of the development of human consciousness. I shall quote the relevant section: '... just as the human individual [in the course of the unfolding of consciousness] initially — by unconsciously using the body as a mirror — awakens to ordinary consciousness of the world without as yet being able to acquire consciousness of his true being, so by finding answers to the challenges to development posed by social life can he in a new way — now experiencing something of his true nature — awaken to the other person. If one focuses upon the progress of human soul-development, the social world represents a kind of metamorphosis of the bodily element. Like the outer world of the senses, it appears before the individual as something given, which — in contrast to the sense-world — in so doing at the same time begins to give expression to what is at first a no more than dimly discernible sense of development which enables the deeper nature of one's fellow men and of him who perceives them to be sensed — albeit not yet fully recognised — in the events of destiny. If this is experienced, the destiny-world of social life begins to become meaningful, to speak to the individual as though out of a preconceived methodology. This can be consciously taken hold of on the path of schooling, so that the spirit-world can be experienced by the individual through the lighting up of visionary consciousness. In the social world, the knowledge acquired through experiencing the sense-world can be reflected on a new level, as a metamorphosis of the bodily element.'* A completely different person from the one who would otherwise be passing through the sense-world awakens within the soul.†

---

* Benedictus Hardorp, *Anthroposophie und Dreigliederung*, Stuttgart 1986, pp.136–47.
† Cf. second note on p.24.

In the awakening capacity for empathy of young adults, of which Urieli reports in his essay, something seems to be springing to conscious life which bears some affinity with early childhood, namely, the sense of basic trust, though now applied in freedom. In the initial awakening of the free power of imagination, the young person can draw the other into his soul-life and may expect that his image also becomes alive in the heart of the other. At the same time, however, we can become aware of the whole vulnerability of this new social faculty, and also of the extent to which it is endangered by those forces which encourage people to gain power over others and — ultimately — influence social life-situations through manipulation of body-bound processes, for example by the media.

During the same period in which the concept of the sense of basic trust gained entry into child psychology in our century, children have been born who were — initially in the USA — described as autistic. They manifested to us the weakening — or what is painfully experienced by their parents as the lack — of the sense of basic trust (as described by Erikson) shortly after birth, with the result that their capacity to imitate was either absent or was deeply submerged. Lorna Wing in England, one of the most experienced researchers in the field of autism in early childhood, has characterised the lack of a 'faculty of imagination' in social life as one of the most obvious symptoms of autistic children and adults. These children appear for what are initially unexplainable reasons in our civilisation under the sign of 'a lost childhood'. But they also document through their destiny the weakening of the power of imagination, whose loss in modern social life was so feared by Rudolf Steiner, and — through this destiny working right into bodily organisation — they warn us of a social impediment to finding ways of building up and fostering a new and hitherto insufficiently developed and understood consciousness for social issues.

In the year 1920 Rudolf Steiner formulated the motto of the social ethic in connection with publications on the social question: 'The healthy social life is found where in the mirror of each human soul the whole community finds its reflection, and where in the community the virtue of each one is living.'* In these words, deriving as they do from the perception of spiritual laws, the path of training described in the present context can be clearly discerned: in imagining, the past is drawn forth from memory forces and made livingly present in the mirror of the human soul. The inclining of the will to the other person creates that free space in which the intuitional powers of the individual come to life; the future arises in social life out of the present spirit-initiative of the individuality.

Wherever such processes begin — in however small a way — to work, a soul-mood deriving from a purified feeling manifests itself amongst those involved as a quality of Inspiration, in which the helping contact with spiritual beings can be dimly experienced if one is attentive to it. Wherever this happens when people are together, the wind of the presence of the spiritual world is blowing.

In the turmoils of daily life, the thinking consciousness must discover the effective potential of the elements of such a social ethic motto in all its simplicity and summon forth the resolution in the soul to develop them through practice. It has been the intention of this essay to draw attention to this need.

---

*Motto inscribed by Rudolf Steiner for Edith Maryon in the book *In Ausführung der Dreigliederung des sozialen Organismus*, Stuttgart 1920. The translation is that of George Adams.

PART TWO

In the universe
Wafts man's essential being.
In the heart of man
Wafts a mirror-picture of the universe.

The ego connects the two
And so fashions
The true meaning of existence.

Notebook entry by Rudolf Steiner, 1918

Baruch Luke Urieli

Cultivating the After-Image Experience

First I should like to emphasise that in my experience fruitful work on experiencing after-images can develop on the right lines only through group-activity. Group-activity is able to bring about that openness and selflessness which provides the key to an experience of the after-image.

The exercises carried out in my seminar begin with attempts to experience the after-image of a coloured surface as radiantly as possible. For example, we begin with attempts to experience the after-image of the coloured surface of a red carpet by first looking at it intently and finally closing our eyes. Then exercises can follow in which we first gaze upon a round surface of a single colour and then transfer our eye to a white surface of a similar size in order to see a clearer after-image (see also M. Mackensen, p.88ff.). There follow exercises with a puzzle picture, where we make ourselves aware that we can look with our eyes from a 'central' or 'peripheral' perspective (see p.10).

A further exercise is the one with the coloured ring described on p.6. Through this exercise one learns to look from a central and peripheral perspective at the same time, thereby obtaining a clear and strong after-image. This establishes the foundation for seeing after-images.

Then we go out into nature and try to experience a tree in the landscape or two completely different trees standing adjacent to one another. Or we contemplate a painted tree in a landscape (for example by Van Goch or Caspar David Friedrich). The after-image experience of the gesture of the tree can reveal a great deal about its nature. As a next step I would include a cat or a dog in the group-activity, and we gradually begin to recognise as a group what the animal's movement reveals about its nature.

Finally, we turn to paintings where a person or group of people is depicted, and we try to describe the inner nature of these people. Or we watch a good film in the evening (on a video) and speak the following morning about what actually happened and showed itself in the after-image. Step by step we learn through all these exercises to discover something about the inner nature of people, groups of people and situations with the help of the after-image experience. It is important that throughout the initial exercises the conscious, selfless way of working is cultivated which is fundamental to all work with the after-image. For a group seeking to learn this for the first time, there is a need both for sufficient time and for the guidance of an experienced person. For younger or inwardly young people, this work is a great experience; for others who want to confine anthroposophy to the intellectual realm or merely 'memorise' Steiner's writings, it is very difficult. To arrive at an experience of the after-image, one needs inner mobility — or at least the longing for it.

Baruch Luke Urieli

Some Observations about the Source-Material on 'Empathy and the After-Image' from the Work of Rudolf Steiner

Approximately in the middle of the second decade of our century, Rudolf Steiner gave his first indications about empathy and the after-image. They were initially associated with the occult school, and appear for example in the lecture of 10 June 1912 from the lecture-cycle *Man in the Light of Occultism, Theosophy and Philosophy*.*

Empathy then appeared in the form in which it became known in Great Britain at that time — that is, as an ability to empathise, which is fundamental for aesthetic enjoyment and artistic creativity (lecture of 15 August 1916 in *The Riddle of Humanity*), and also as the capacity to perceive the thinking of the other person (the first appendix to *The Philosophy of Freedom*).

In 1918 Rudolf Steiner drew attention to some important connections, how 'karma and after-image exercises' lead in the context of one's own biography to new social capacities and moral qualities, as in the lecture of 19 March 1918 in *Earthly Death and Cosmic Life* and in the lecture of 12 December 1918 ('Social and Anti-Social Forces in the Human Being'). Finally, Rudolf Steiner spoke at some length about the after-image as the foundation of a Michael culture in the lecture of 30 November 1919 (*The Mission of the Archangel Michael*), three months after he had, in the lecture of 29 August 1919 (*The Study of Man*), fully described the sense of ego first mentioned in 1916 in *Towards Imagi-*

---

*Further bibliographical details can be found before the quoted texts in the collection of source material.

nation (GA 169); and it thereby became apparent that the sense of ego is that sense which has the capacity to 'imitate' empathetically the ego of one's fellow human being.

As far as the after-image is concerned, the year 1919 was of decisive importance in Rudolf Steiner's creative work. This is apparent from another, less well-known lecture, where he spoke in detail about the after-image: that of 10 November 1919.

Hans Müller-Wiedemann has in his essay drawn fully upon this lecture, which was particularly intended for those who were seeking foundations for a renewal of social life.

However, this was by no means the end of Rudolf Steiner's work with empathy and the after-image. In a lecture of 27 May 1922 (*The Human Soul in Relation to World Evolution*), he described from the standpoint of spiritual schooling the new 'yoga will' which he had characterised in the lecture of 30 November 1919 as a 'light-soul-process'. Finally, in the lectures of 23 November 1923 and 9 December 1923 (*Mystery Knowledge and Mystery Centres*) and in that of 13 January 1924 (*Rosicrucianism and Modern Initiation*), he showed how the path that begins with experiencing the after-image of a physical colour leads by way of empathy and after-image of plant, animal and man to the sense of ego, so as then to gain entry to the new Mysteries.

In order to take this fifth step of entering the new Mysteries, it would be necessary to work through the lecture of 7 March 1914 (*Pre-Earthly Deeds of Christ*) and ask oneself what the new memory described there actually is. However, this step, which leads to the destiny-experience of the future, lies beyond the scope of this book.

Collection of Source Material from Writings and Lectures by Rudolf Steiner

1. *From:* Man in the Light of Occultism, Theosophy and Philosophy, *GA 137, lecture of 10 June 1912*

(Translation revised from that published anonymously by Rudolf Steiner Press in 1964)

I should now like to give you a picture of what happens when a pupil in occultism, taking the human form as his starting-point, penetrates into the supersensible world. I do not know whether any of you will have observed in yourselves a remarkable experience that happens every day but has to be quite consciously observed if one wants to gain knowledge from it. I mean the experience that when you have directed your gaze especially upon a bright object, the impression remains in the eye after the eye has ceased looking at it. Goethe made a very special study – as he tells us repeatedly in his *Theory of Colours* – of these after-images that remain behind in the organism, that is, inside the human form. When, for example, you lie down in bed, put out the light and shut your eyes, you can continue to have before you an image of the light as a kind of echo. For most people who have experienced this 'echoing', the external impression is over once the echoing has ceased. The movements or vibrations caused by the outward impression have finished, and for most people it has then come to an end.

In this respect too the pupil must take the human form as his starting-point, that is, what we know the human form to be on the physical plane in ordinary life. So long as he observes only the after-images, nothing of importance will happen. The interest begins only when something still remains once the after-image has gone. For what then remains no longer comes from the eye; rather is it a process, an experience that is given to us by the etheric body. Anyone who has himself carried out this experiment will not make the perfectly reasonable objection that this too could only be an after-image of the physical body. People say this only if they have not experienced it themselves. Once they have had the experience, they stop saying it. For what remains is something totally different from anything that has an outward physical relationship to the external impression.

In most cases, what remains after an impression of colour or light is by no means the illusion of light or colour. Indeed, we can say that if it is colour or light, then it is illusion! It is a *tone*, though one is quite certain that it did not derive in any way from the ear. It can be thought of as another impression, but it is always different from the external impression. The occultist must get used to completely overcoming external impressions, for occultism is also for the blind, for example, who have never in their life seen an external object, never once had any external impression of light by means of the eye. Most of the ghostlike figures that people see are merely memory-pictures of sense-impressions that have been changed by the play of fancy. Occult experience is not dependent on whether a person can use some particular sense-organ or not; it occurs quite independently of the sense-organs.

2. *From:* The Riddle of Humanity, *GA 170, lecture of 15 August 1916*

(Translation based on that of John Logan, Rudolf Steiner Press 1990.)

In this way three new soul-faculties arise. In character they resemble — but are not identical with — the earthly faculties of thinking, feeling and will, and likewise have a threefold aspect. These faculties are something other than earthly thinking, feeling and will. They are more like life-processes, but not so differentiated as the life-processes of the earth. When someone is able to sustain this sinking back into [Old] Moon without lapsing into visions, a very intimate, subtle process takes place. The sensory regions are transformed into regions of life, the life-processes into soul-processes, and there arises a kind of understanding that is faintly suggestive of the Old Moon visions. Nor can a person remain constantly in this state, for then one would cease to be fit for life on earth. To be fit for the earth one needs the kind of senses and vital organs we have described previously. But in certain circumstances a person can enter into this other state. Then, if the state tends more towards the will, it leads to aesthetic creation; if the state tends more towards perception, it leads to aesthetic enjoyment. The truly aesthetic aspect of human behaviour consists in that the sense-organs are enlivened in a certain way and the life-processes ensouled. This is an extremely important truth about humanity; it explains much. That life of the sense-organs and sense-regions which is more vigorous than, and of a different nature from, what is ordinarily the case is to be found in art and in the enjoyment of art. Something similar occurs with the life-processes, which are more ensouled in the enjoyment of art than they are in normal life. Because these things are not considered in their true light in our materialistic age, the significance of the changes a person undergoes when he is involved with art cannot be understood in their entirety. Today a human being is seen as concrete and fixed. But, within certain limits, people actually are variable. This is demonstrated by the sort of variability we have just been considering.

3. *From:* The Philosophy of Freedom, *GA 4, Appendix 1*

(The translation given here is essentially that of Michael Wilson, published by Rudolf Steiner Press in 1964.)

This problem, which has been created by several recent tendencies in epistemology, can be clarified if one tries to survey the matter from the point of view of the spiritually orientated observation adopted in this book. What is it, in the first instance, that I have before me when I confront another person? The most immediate thing is the bodily appearance of the other person as given to me in sense-perception; then, perhaps, the auditory perception of what he is saying, and so on. I do not merely stare at all this, but it sets my thinking activity in motion. Through the thinking with which I confront the other person, the percept becomes, as it were, transparent to the mind. I am bound to admit that when I grasp the percept with my thinking, it is not at all the same thing as appeared to the outer senses. In what appears directly to the senses, something else is indirectly revealed. The mere sense-appearance ex-tinguishes itself at the same time as it confronts me. But what it reveals through this extinguishing compels me as a thinking being to extinguish my own thinking as long as I am under its influence, and to put *its* thinking in the place of mine. I then grasp *its* thinking in my thinking as an experience like my own. I have really perceived another person's thinking. The immediate percept, extinguishing itself as sense-appearance, is grasped by my thinking, and this is a process lying wholly within my consciousness and consisting in this, that the other person's thinking takes the place of mine. Through the self-extinction of the sense-appearance, the separation between the two spheres of consciousness is actually overcome. This expresses itself in my consciousness as little as I experience it in dreamless sleep. Just as in dreamless sleep my waking consciousness is eliminated, so in my perceiving of the content of another person's consciousness the content of my own is eliminated. The illusion that it is not so only comes about because in perceiving the other person, firstly, the extinction of the content of one's own consciousness gives place not to unconsciousness, as it does in sleep, but to the content of the other person's consciousness, and secondly, the alternations between extinguishing and lighting up again of my own self-consciousness follow too rapidly to be generally noticed.

This whole problem is to be solved, not through artificial conceptual structures with inferences from the conscious to things that can never become conscious, but rather through genuine experience of what results from combining thinking with the percept. This applies to a great many problems which appear in philosophical literature. Thinkers should seek the path to open-minded, spiritually orientated observation; instead of which they insert an artificial conceptual structure between themselves and reality.

4. *From:* Earthly Death and Cosmic Life, *GA 181, lecture of 19 March 1918*

(Translation revised from that published by Rudolf Steiner Press in 1964, which was itself a revision by Charles Davy and Dorothy Osmond.)

This too is the basis of our karma; our karma arises from it. From this subconscious feeling, which at first emerges in a nebulous way, we have the general feeling of oneness with the world. Because we do indeed leave our mark everywhere, we have this general sense of oneness with the world. We can catch hold of it, sense it, perceive it. In order to do this, however, we must pay attention to certain intimacies of life. We must try, for instance, really to enter into the idea, 'I am now crossing a street'; we then walk across, and afterwards we still imagine ourselves crossing it. By continued exercises of this kind, we call forth from the depths of our soul a general feeling of oneness with the world. For anyone who becomes more clearly conscious of this sense of oneness, it develops in such a way that he ultimately says to himself: there is after all a connection, albeit an invisible one, with all things, as between the members of a single organism. As each finger, each lobe of the ear, everything belonging to our organism, has a connection with the other parts, so is there a connection between all things and all that happens, in so far as the occurrences take place in our world.

Earthly human beings of today have as yet no fully valid consciousness of this sense of oneness with all things, this organic penetration into things; it remains in the unconscious. In the Jupiter evolution this feeling will be the fundamental one, and as we gradually make our way from the fifth to the sixth post-Atlantean epoch we are preparing for this. But the cultivation of this feeling is necessary also for the present and the immediate future; it must come to furnish humanity with a moral foundation that is much more alive than is anything of the kind today.

I mean, for example, that many people today think nothing of enriching themselves at the expense of others. Moreover, not only do they live at others' expense without any moral self-criticism; they simply do not think about it at all. Were they to reflect about it, they would find that a person lives far more at the cost of others than they had ever realised. Indeed, everyone lives at the expense of others. People will come to realise that a life lived at the expense of others signifies the same for a community as when a particular organ develops at the expense of another organ in an illegitimate way, and that the welfare of the individual is not really possible apart from that of the community.

Today, of course, there is no inkling of this; but it must gradually become the fundamental principle of true human ethics. People today strive for their own welfare, not thinking that their own welfare is fundamentally possible only with that of everyone else.

There is therefore a connection between the sense of oneness of which I have spoken and the feeling that the life of the whole community is an organism. This feeling can be very greatly enhanced within the individual. He can develop an intimate sense of togetherness with the things around him. If he fosters this intimate feeling, he gradually becomes able to receive a perception of what I described in the previous lecture as the 'light' which is cast beyond death into our evolution between death and rebirth, a light which we perceive and out of which we form our karma.

5. *From:* Social and Anti-Social Forces in Man, *a lecture given on 12 December 1918 (GA 186)*

(Translation based on Christopher Schaefer's revision published by Mercury Press in 1982.)

I should like to discuss one question from the viewpoint of general education, namely: How can we consciously establish social impulses to balance those anti-social forces which are developing naturally within us? How can we cultivate them in such a way that the interest that one person takes in another, a quality which has become so drastically eroded in our consciousness-soul age, springs up in us, develops further and further and leaves us no peace? In our age veritable chasms have already been created between people—to the extent that they have no idea of the way that they pass one another by without in the least comprehending one another. The desire to understand the other in all his or her uniqueness is very weak today. On the one hand we have the call for social principles and on the other the ever-growing disintegrating force of a purely anti-social instinct. The blindness of people towards each other can be seen in the many clubs and societies which they form. It very rarely happens that these provide any opportunity for them to get to know one another. People today can be in others' company for years and know them no better than they did when they first met them. What is necessary is that in future the social should be brought to meet the anti-social in a systematic way. For this there are various inner methods. One is that now and then we try to look back over our present life, our present incarnation, to survey what has happened in this life between us and those whom we have encountered. If we are honest in this, most of us will say: nowadays we generally regard this entering of all these people into our lives in such a way that we place ourselves in the centre of our life's review. What have we gained from this or that person who has come into our life? This is our natural way of feeling. It is exactly this which we must try to combat. We should try to allow a picture to appear before our souls of the individuals who as teachers, friends or otherwise have helped us, and also of those who have caused us hurt (to whom from a certain point of view we often owe more than those who have been of use to us). We should try to allow these pictures to pass before our souls as vividly as possible in order to see what each has done for us; and if we do this we shall see that by degrees we learn to forget ourselves, that we find that actually almost everything which forms part of us could not be there at all unless this or that person had affected our lives, helping us or teaching us something. Only when we look back over the more distant past, recalling people with whom we may no longer be in contact and about whom it is easier to be objective, do we see how the soul-substance of our lives has been created by what has exerted an influence on us. Our gaze then extends over a multitude of people whom we have known in the course of time. If we try to develop a sense of the debt we owe to this or that person, if we try to see ourselves in the mirror of those who have influenced us in the course of time and who have been associated with us, we shall then be able to experience the opening-up of a new sense in our souls. Through our having cultivated forming pictures of those people who have been connected with us in the past, a sense is released from our soul which enables us also to gain a picture of those whom we meet in the present, with whom we stand face to face today. It is of tremendous importance that the impulse awakens in us not merely to feel sympathy or antipathy towards the people we meet, not merely to hate or love something about the other person, but to awaken a true picture of the other in us that is free from love or hate.

Perhaps you will not feel that what I am saying is of any great importance. It is enormously important. For this ability to make a picture of the other person present within oneself without love or hate, allowing the other individual to be resurrected within oneself, is a quality which with every week in human evolution is — I would say — more or less disappearing, it is something which people are gradually completely losing. They pass one another by without the impulse being aroused in them to awaken to the other person. Yet this is something that must be consciously cultivated. This ability to develop this imaginative capacity in man is also something which must enter into pedagogy and the education of children. For we can indeed develop this imaginative faculty if, instead of striving after the immediate sensations of life as is often done today, we are not afraid to look back quietly in our soul and view our past connections with others. We thereby gradually also begin to acquire an imaginative relationship to those individuals whom we meet in the present. In this way we develop a social impulse to counterbalance the anti-social impulse which quite unconsciously and of necessity continues to grow.

6. *From:* The Study of Man, *GA 293, lecture of 29 August 1919*

(Translation essentially that of Daphne Harwood and Helen Fox, as revised by A.C. Harwood and published by Rudolf Steiner Press in 1966.)

When a person thinks of his conception of the ego, he thinks at once of his own soul-being and that usually satisfies him. Psychologists do almost the same thing. They do not consider in the least that it is one thing if I describe as 'I' all that I experience as myself, the sum indeed of this experience, and that it is a completely different thing when I meet someone and through the kind of relationship I have with him describe *him* as an ego, an 'I'. These are two quite different activities of the soul and spirit. In the first instance when I sum up the activities of my life in the comprehensive synthesis 'I', I have something purely inward; in the second instance when I meet another person and through my relationship to him discover that he too is something of the same kind as my ego, I have an activity before me which takes place in the interplay between me and the other person.* Hence I must realise that perceiving my own ego within me is something different from recognising another person as an ego. The perceiving of the other ego depends upon the *ego-sense* just as the perceiving of colour depends upon the sense of sight, and the perceiving of sound upon the sense of hearing. The organ of seeing is open to our sight, but nature does not make it so easy for someone to see

---

*See the Appendix added by Rudolf Steiner in 1918 to *The Philosophy of Freedom*.

the organ that perceives the ego. But we might well use the word 'to ego' [German: *ichen*] for the perceiving of other 'I's or egos as we use the word 'to see' for the perceiving of colour. The organ for the perceiving of colour is external to man; the organ for the perceiving of egos is spread out over the whole human being and consists of a very fine substantiality, and on this account people do not talk about this 'organ for perceiving the ego'. And this 'organ for perceiving the ego' is a different thing from that whereby I experience my own ego. There is indeed a vast difference between experiencing my own ego and perceiving the ego in another. For the perceiving of the ego of another is essentially a process of knowledge, at least a process which is similar to knowledge, whereas experiencing one's own ego is a process of will.

We have now come to the point where a pedant might feel very pleased. He might say: yesterday you said that the activities of all the senses were pre-eminently activities of the will; now you construe the sense of ego and say that it is principally a sense of knowledge. But if you characterise the sense of ego as I have tried to do in the new edition of my *Philosophy of Freedom* you will realise that this sense of ego really works in a very complicated way. On what does the perceiving of the ego of the other person really depend? The theorists of the present day say things that are quite extraordinary. They say: you see the form of the outward human being, you hear his voice, and moreover you know that you look human yourself like the other, and that you have within you a being who thinks and feels and wills, who is thus also a man of soul and spirit. So you conclude by analogy: as there is in me a thinking, feeling and willing being, so is there also in the other person. This conclusion by analogy is simply foolishness. The interrelationship between the one person and the other contains something quite different. When you confront another person, something like the following happens. You perceive him for a short time; he makes an impression on you. This impression disturbs you inwardly; you feel that this individual, who is really a being similar to yourself, is making an impression on you like an attack. The result is that you 'defend' yourself in your inner being, that you oppose yourself to this attack, that you become inwardly aggressive towards him. This feeling abates and your aggression ceases; hence he can now make another impression on you. Then your force of aggression has time to surface again, and again you have an aggressive feeling. Once more it abates and the other makes a fresh impression on you and so on. That is the relationship which exists when one person meets another and perceives his ego: giving yourself up to the other human being—inwardly warding him off; giving yourself up again—warding him off; sympathy—antipathy; sympathy—antipathy. I am not now speaking of the feeling life, but of what takes place in perception when you confront someone. The soul vibrates: sympathy—antipathy; sympathy—antipathy; they vibrate too (you can read this in the new edition of *The Philosophy of Freedom*).

This however is not all. In that sympathy is active, you sleep into the other human being; in that antipathy is active, you wake up again, and so on. There is this quick alternation in vibrations between waking and sleeping when we meet another person. We owe this alternation to the organ of the sense of ego. Thus this organ for the perception of the ego is organised in such a way that it apprehends the ego of another by means of a sleeping, not a waking will and then quickly carries over this apprehension accomplished in sleep to the region of knowledge, i.e. to the nervous system. Thus when we view the matter truly, the principal thing in the perception of another person is after all the will, but essentially a will which acts in a state of sleep, not waking. For we are constantly weaving moments of sleep into the act of perceiving another ego. What lies between them is indeed knowledge that is immediately carried over into the domain of the nervous system. So that I can really call the perceiving of another a process of knowledge, but I must know that this process of knowledge is only a metamorphosis of a sleeping will-organ. Thus this sense-process is really a process of the will, only we do not recognise it as such. We do not experience in conscious life all the knowledge which we experience in sleep.

7. *From:* The Mission of the Archangel Michael, GA 194, *the lectures of 30 November and 7 December 1919*

(The translation of the first lecture is a revised version of that by Lisa D. Monges, published by Anthroposophic Press in 1961. The second lecture is available in translation only in typescript form — Z 415, available from the Library, Rudolf Steiner House, London — and reference has been made to this.)

When our sense-processes have become ensouled again, we shall have established a crossing-point, and at this crossing-point we shall take hold of the human will that streams up out of the third stratum of consciousness, as I have described it to you in the past few days. Then we shall at the same time have the interplay between subject and object for which Goethe was longing so very much. We shall again become able to gain a sensitive understanding of how remarkable the process actually is whereby man relates to the outer world through his senses. The idea that the outer world simply has an affect on us to which we then merely react is a thoroughly crude one. People talk a great deal of nonsense of this kind. What actually happens is that a soul-process takes place working from without inwards, which is grasped by the deeply subconscious, inner soul-process in such a way that the two processes intersect. Cosmic thoughts stream into us from without, human will reaches out from within. Human will and cosmic thought intersect at this crossing-point, just as the objective and subjective elements once crossed in the breath. We must learn to feel how our will works through our eyes and how the activity of the senses delicately mingles with their passivity, bringing about the crossing of cosmic thoughts and human will. We must develop this new yoga will. Something will then be imparted to us that is of like nature to that which was imparted to human beings in the breathing process three millennia ago. Our understanding must become much more soul-like, much more spiritual.

Goethe's world-conception aimed in this direction. Goethe sought to recognise the pure phenomenon, which he called the primal phenomenon; he wove together in his mind only what works upon man in the external world and did not mix this up with the luciferic thoughts stemming from man's head. These thoughts were merely to serve to weave the phenomena together. Goethe aspired to find not the laws of nature but the primal phenomena. This is what was significant about him. If, however, we arrive at this pure phenomenon, this primal phenomenon, we have something in the world outside of us which makes it possible for us to feel in addition the unfolding of our will as we behold the outer world; and then we shall bring ourselves back to an interplay between subject and object, as was still present for example in the ancient Hebrew teachings. We must learn not merely to speak of the contrast between the material and the spiritual, but we must recognise the interplay of the material and the spiritual as brought together precisely in sense-perception. If we no longer look at nature purely materially and, moreover, if we do not imagine into it a soul-element, as Gustav Theodor Fechner did, something will arise which will signify for us what the Yahveh culture signified for mankind three millennia ago. If in nature we learn to receive the soul-element together with sense-perception, we shall have the Christ-relationship to outer nature. This Christ-relationship to outer nature will be something like a kind of spiritual breathing process.

We shall be aided by realising more and more—though now through exercising our healthy human intelligence—that pre-existence lies at the foundation of our soul-life. We must supplement the purely egoistic notion of 'post-existence', which springs merely from our longing to exist after death, by the knowledge of the pre-existence of the soul. We must again rise to the view that the soul is indeed eternal. This is what may be called the Michael culture. If we go through the world with the awareness that with every glance that we cast, every tone that we hear, something spiritual (or at any rate something of a soul nature) streams into us, and that at the same time we radiate a soul-element into the world, we have gained the consciousness that mankind needs for the future.

I shall return once more to the image. You see a flame. You shut your eyes and have the after-image, which fades. Is that merely a subjective process? Yes, says the modern physiologist. But this is not true. In the cosmic ether this signifies an objective process, just as in the air the presence of carbonic acid which you exhale signifies an objective process. You impress into the cosmic ether the image which you only sense as a fading after-image. This is not merely subjective, it is an objective process. You are dealing here with something objective. Here you have the possibility of recognising that something which is taking place within you is at the same time in a finer sense a cosmic process, if you but become conscious of it in this way. If I look at a flame, close my eyes, let it fade—it will fade even if I keep my eyes open, only then I will not notice it—I am experiencing a process which is not merely taking place within me, it is taking place in the world. But this is not only the case with regard to the flame. If I confront a human being and say: this person has said this or that, which may be true or untrue, this constitutes a judgement, a moral or intellectual act of my inner nature. This fades away like the flame. It is an objective world process. If you think something good about your fellow man, it fades away and is an objective process in the cosmic ether; if you think something bad, it fades away as an objective process. You are unable to conceal your perceptions and judgements about the world in some little room. You might seem to be carrying them about with you, but they are at the same time an objective world process. Just as people of the third epoch were conscious of the fact that the breathing process is something which takes place simultaneously within man and in the objective world, so mankind must become aware that the soul-quality of which I have spoken is at the same time an objective world process.

This transformation of consciousness demands greater strength of soul than is ordinarily developed by the human being of today. Filling ourselves with this consciousness will inaugurate the Michael culture. To the extent that we conceive of light as being the general representative of sense-perception, we must bring ourselves to think of light as ensouled — just as it was self-evident for people of the second and third pre-Christian millennia to think of the air as ensouled (as indeed it was). We must thoroughly overcome the habit of viewing light in the way that our materialistic age is accustomed to do. We must completely banish the notion that only those vibrations of which modern physics and the general consciousness of humanity speak today emanate from the sun. We must become clear that soul pours through cosmic space on pinions of light. At the same time we must realise that this was not the case in the period preceding our age. In this age prior to our own, what comes to us now through light approached mankind through the air. You see here an objective difference in the earth-process. Expressing this in a comprehensive concept,

we may say: air-soul-process, light-soul-process. This is
what may be observed in the evolution of the Earth. And in
between the two, as the transition from one to the other,
falls the Mystery of Golgotha.

Mystery of Golgotha

Air-soul-process   Light-soul-process

It will not be adequate for the present and future of
mankind to waffle abstractly about the spiritual, to fall into
some sort of nebulous pantheism; on the contrary, it is
necessary that what people today experience as a purely
material process is recognised at least to some extent as
being imbued with soul-forces.

We need to learn to speak along these lines: there was a
time prior to the Mystery of Golgotha when the earth had
an atmosphere which contained the soul-element that
belongs to the soul of man. Today, the earth has an atmosphere which is devoid of this soul-element. Instead, that
soul-element which was previously in the air has now
entered into the light which encompasses us from morning
until evening. This has been made possible through Christ's
uniting Himself with the earth. From a soul-spiritual aspect
too, therefore, air and light have undergone a change in the
course of Earth evolution.

It is childish to describe air and light from a similar, and
purely material, point of view for the duration of the millennia of Earth evolution. Air and light have changed
inwardly. We live in an atmosphere and a light-sphere that
are different from those in which our souls lived in previous
earthly incarnations. What matters is to learn to recognise
the outwardly material as of a soul-spiritual nature. We will
not arrive at a real spiritual science if on the one hand
people describe purely material existence in the customary
manner and then add, as a kind of decoration: in this

material existence the spiritual is also to be found every-where! People are very strange in this respect; where these things are concerned they are intent on withdrawing into abstractions. What is necessary is, however, that in future we stop differentiating abstractly between the material and the spiritual and instead seek the spiritual in the material itself and, moreover, describe it for what it is; and that in the spiritual we recognise the transition to the material, its way of working in the material domain. Only if we have attained this shall we be able to gain a true knowledge of man. 'Blood is a quite special fluid'; but what physiologists talk about today is not a special fluid at all, it is simply a fluid whose chemical composition one attempts to analyse like any other chemical compound — it is nothing special. But once we have arrived at the starting-point of being able to grasp the metamorphosis of air and light in its soul aspect, we shall gradually advance to a soul-spiritual under-standing of man himself in all his individual members; then we shall no longer have abstract matter and abstract spirit but spirit, soul and body working into one another. This will be Michael culture.

7 December 1919
As is essential for our inner integrity as human beings, we retain a picture in our memory of what we have thus experienced through our senses, of what we have thought out by means of our so-called reasoning intelligence; and it is ultimately this memory-picture which we retain from what we have initially received from the outside world by way of our senses and have made something out of through our intelligence. But what is it to us that we as human beings confront the world in the way I have described?

Let us take our start from a simple phenomenon of sense-perception to which I drew your attention a few days ago. You see a flame by means of your eyes. You close your eyes; and you have an after-image of the flame. This after-image

of the flame which you have in your eye gradually disappears. Goethe, who always expressed himself graphically
in such matters, speaks of it as echoing away. The original
constitution of the eye and of the nerve-organisation
associated with it is re-established after being modified by
the impression which the light made upon it. What takes
place in your sense-organ is but the simpler equivalent of
what goes on in your memory when you take in outward
impressions in general, think them over and retain them as
memory-pictures. The difference is simply that when your
eye receives an impression of—let us say—a flame, you
have the mental picture of the flame which then dies away
again, it lasts only a short time. But when you receive an
impression with the whole of you, think it over and are later
able to recall it again, this larger after-image of a memory
lasts a long time—it may under certain conditions even last
all your life. What is the reason for this? If the simple after-
image that you have in your eye lives on for only a few
minutes or perhaps less than a minute before it fades, this is
only because it does not go through your whole organism
but remains in a part of it. That which becomes a memory-
picture goes through a considerable part—I shall presently
describe it in more detail—of your entire organism, thrusts
its way into the etheric body and from thence into the
surrounding ether. The moment when an image does not
merely remain as a sensory image in an individual organ
but passes through a considerable part of the whole human
being, impresses itself on the etheric body and thrusts its
way outward, it can remain as an after-image for one's
whole life. The point is that the impression must go deep
enough and take hold of the etheric body, and that the
etheric body does not retain it but transmits it to the outer
ether of the cosmos and inscribes it there. Do not suppose
that when you remember things this is merely a process
taking place within you. It is true that you cannot always
write up what you experience in your note-book and read it

again afterwards — although a number of people today do that with many of their experiences. But what you remember you inscribe in the cosmic ether, and the cosmic ether summons it forth in you again like the impress of a seal when you call it to mind. Memory is no mere personal affair; through it you relate yourself to the entire universe. You cannot be alone if, as someone with an inner hold on himself, you seek to remember your experiences. If a person does not remember his experiences, this destroys his very being.

8. *From:* Die Befreiung des Menschenwesens als Grundlage für eine soziale Neugestaltung *('The Freeing of Man's Being as the Foundation for a New Social Order'), GA 329, the lecture of 10 November 1919*

(Newly translated.)

When Goethe was travelling through Italy in order to bring clarity and greater maturity to his conception of the world, he wrote to his Weimar friends, who were well aware of what he had in mind with his archetypal plant, that this conception of his was brought back to him particularly strongly by the rich, exuberant plant-world of Italy. Beginning in an abstract way — though we shall soon see that there is no need to confine ourselves to an abstract view of the matter — he says: Such an archetypal plant must surely exist, for how otherwise could people recognise that each individual representative of the whole manifold plant kingdom is indeed a plant? As I have said, this is abstractly expressed; but Goethe goes on to speak far more concretely and forcefully about this archetypal plant. Thus he says, for example: If one has grasped the idea of this archetypal plant with one's mind, one can then out of such an image form for oneself pictures of actual individual plants which have the possibility of existing.

One needs only to consider aright what is actually being said by means of such words. Thus Goethe is seeking to develop in his mind an idea of the nature of plants in general, and he wants to have the possibility of forming a conception out of his archetypal plant which is an individual plant — not, however, a plant which he sees with his senses but which, as it were, adds to such plants one that does not exist as a sense-perceptible reality but nevertheless could potentially exist given the necessary conditions. What is actually being spoken of here? It is that man can in his soul dive down into sense-perceptible reality and experience thereby the spiritual aspect of sense-perceptible phenomena in such a way that he grows together with this spirit creatively living and weaving everywhere in nature.

That is the greatness of Goethe's way of looking at the world — that it is directed towards this diving down into reality and has the conviction that, insofar as one dives down into this reality, one arrives at its spiritual aspect and thus discovers the spirit inherent within it, which can be a guide through the whole confusing diversity of the sense-perceptible world itself...

As you know, in the course of living in the world we perceive it through our senses and then we assimilate it. This is also of course what ordinary science does. We assimilate this world by thinking about it, laying bare its laws and forming mental pictures or ideas about it. You also know that this forming of mental pictures leads to something else, to something that is intimately connected with the health of our personal human nature. This forming of mental pictures about the world is associated with the fact that we are able to retain the impressions of the world through what we would call our memory, our faculty of remembering. People tend very easily to omit this faculty from their consideration, on the grounds that it seems so everyday. But this is precisely what is characteristic of a real aspiration for knowledge—that what may indeed be of an everyday nature must be conceived of by us as that in accordance with which the most important and significant questions must be opened up.

When we perceive the world of the senses, form mental pictures about it and after a time seemingly bring it forth again from ourselves, so that we recall the experiences that we have had, there is much that is unconscious about the process of remembering. Just think how little you are the master of your memory, how lacking your faculty of remembering can be. Consider above all how little you are able to think about this process of remembering while you are engaged in outward perception. Or is it, rather, the case that, as we look at the world with our eyes and hear tones with our ears, we are at the same time making sure that there are the mental pictures which make it possible for us to recall everything? No, we would have to be consciously exercising another power apart from that of perception, apart from the workings of our senses. In ordinary life we do not do this. I would say that memory and its power functions alongside outward life. But it works sub-consciously, in a certain sense exerting an influence on all life in the outer world of the senses, so that we carry this life with us in our lives by virtue of our memory. It is drawn forth from our subconscious as a power. In other words: we cannot draw forth what we cultivate unconsciously as our faculty of memory out of the depths of our soul simply by recalling our experiences; rather can we do this by trying to bring that power of memory which we otherwise hardly know—and which, as I say, functions alongside our experiences—to a conscious clarity such as is characteristic only of our outward perceptions, by drawing this power forth from unconscious depths and by living in what otherwise resides in the subconscious realm of memory. If we use our power of memory not in order to remember as such but so that the ideas and mental pictures which are otherwise kept alive only through the power of memory may be allowed to remain consciously present in our mind, we strengthen something in our mind through which we may — when the necessary time for this has arrived — come to know of a quite different kind of awakening from that which we experience every morning. If one again and again consciously works in a way that otherwise only the faculty of memory does, one experiences something of a new awakening in one's soul. One experiences something akin to the opening up of a completely different person in one's soul from the one who makes his way through the world of the senses. The spirit cannot be reached by theorising about it. Philosophical debates which seek to arrive at the spirit purely through following a line of reasoning do not actually have anything in view other than talking about the spirit. The spirit wants to be experienced. And it can be experienced only if we uplift the activity of memory — which is otherwise deeply unconscious and lives at deeper levels of our human psyche — so that it lives within us with a light-filled clarity similar to that which we see with our eyes and hear with our ears, and so that in this process the conscious will lives in the way that it does when I turn my eye from this wall to that wall in order to look away from what I am seeing here to what I can see there. In that I make use of my senses, my conscious will lives in this process. This inner work of the soul must be wholly imbued with this will; and we will then arrive at what amounts to a continuation of our ordinary soul-activity in the same way that the waking life of day relates to sleep-life, which we know only through our dreams.

The faculty in human nature which can be uplifted to become a new organ of cognition and which Goethe calls the eye of the soul, the spirit-eye, is what anthroposophically orientated spiritual science would seek to bring to manifestation through a gradual focusing upon such inner work of the soul. In this way it would give expression to what ordinary science is unable to express, because it lives under the pressure that has been indicated. However, because humanity has a longing for it (this longing can be observed, if one can only be sufficiently unprejudiced), this pressure needs to be removed from human knowledge.

So you see that anthroposophically orientated spiritual science does not seek to be some kind of crazy mysticism, not something obscure, but a true continuation of what can be known through ordinary science. Anyone who has enjoyed a scientific education will find it easier to concentrate and meditate on thoughts; for he has grown accustomed to methods, to modes of research, which reject subjectivity in favour of objectivity. If one directs the qualities that one has developed through ordinary science towards meditation, one divests oneself of all human arbitrariness and brings something into meditation, into one's inner soul-activity, which is akin to the objective laws of nature herself. By adopting the methods of thinking and cognition proper to ordinary science, one will overcome the chaotic, unclear form of self-knowledge which is striven for in much mysticism of the daft and muddled variety, where people wish merely to brood over their own inner selves. Against this tendency to brood there stands that work upon oneself which with every step proceeds in a way that is worthy only of the most conscientious scientist, who extends his power of judgement over what is spread out before his eyes or his instruments.

That is the one aspect. I would say that it is the aspect that points towards the awakening of particular cognitive powers. The ordinary faculty of memory will of course not be present in such moments when one seeks to explore the spiritual directly, since this faculty has in such a case itself undergone a metamorphosis. It has become a spirit-eye which can perceive the spirit. With the ordinary kind of reasoning characteristic of the logic that has currency today, it is not possible truly to reach forward to the spirit. Anyone wishing to speak about a real advance towards the spirit must necessarily address the powers leading to the spirit which actually exist. Such a power is the faculty of memory. However, this faculty of memory must be transformed and become something entirely different. Any other path of entry into the spirit leads at the same time into the darkness, because the human will is thereby excluded and — with it — the most important part of man's being. Just as we do not regard as true memory the fantasy life welling up from the depths of our mind over which we have no control, so will the spirit-researcher not accept for his research any soul-content which he does not wholly penetrate with the light of his will.

So much for the one aspect, the activity of mental picturing as it is applied in spiritual research. But there is something else in man that must also be made use of if one really wants to find the path into the supersensible, into the spiritual world. And just as spiritual science is challenged by the way that ideas are formed today out of the spirit of ordinary natural science, so in another sense is spiritual science challenged by the way modern human life is lived. Anyone who traces the evolution of the human soul through the last few centuries impartially and without the prejudices of a modern historian would be able to say that around the middle of the fifteenth century a mighty upheaval came about in the constitution of human souls, only in the civilised world, to be sure, but quite expressly within this world. It is a mere prejudice if, in considering only the outward historical facts, one believes a human soul of the civilised world in the eighth and ninth centuries AD to have had the same inner constitution as do human souls today. To be sure, there are also people today who are behind the times and who are still more or less in the eighth or ninth centuries; but they are of great interest, because they lead us in an outward sense back to those times. Nevertheless, all in all we may say: one needs only to examine human life in accordance with one's experience. An immense upheaval has taken place which since the middle of the fifteenth century has manifested itself more and more strongly. If we would describe it more precisely, we would have to say: as one goes beyond this point, one finds that people related to one another completely differently than is the case today and as unconscious powers are seeking to guide mankind into the future. Whatever one may say to the contrary out of certain prejudices, something was being striven for with regard to the relation between one person and another that had its beginning at the time indicated. At the earlier time people were close to one another through blood-relationships and racial kinship, through everything that gave them a relationship to other people by virtue of their organism, or through other relationships of an organic nature (such as sexual love, for instance). Can we not see—if we did but want to do so—that there is an increasing tendency for the old blood ties and family relationships to be replaced by what works from one person to another, that something reaches from the willing soul of one person to the willing soul of another? Can we not see that modern trends of development make it increasingly necessary for one person to approach another person through something altogether different from his mere bodily organism? We do indeed see that the consciousness of personality has been growing since the time indicated, that people have been becoming more and more inward and also more and more lonely. Since this time, I would say, the soul-life of the individual has been growing more and more isolated. The life of the soul is closing off from the outside world. Blood no longer speaks when we confront those closest to us in this sense. We have to stir ourselves inwardly. We have to live into the other. In a soul sense we have to become completely absorbed in the other. Particularly in those circles which with justice call themselves socialist, there is a grave misunderstanding of what might be called the social principle, the social impulse of modern times. This social impulse can be seen emerging, but only in the most limited circles do people know of what it consists.

It consists in that it happens all the more often that the impulse stirs in us solitary individuals of today to reach in a soul-spiritual sense through our will into other people, so that the person closest to us is so by virtue not of blood or organic relationship but of consciousness. In such a case we confront other people and have the need to 'live into' them. What we call wishing someone well, what we today call love, is somewhat different from what people referred to in this way in former times. But in so far as we enter into the other person in this way, it is as though everything that pulsates in us, that lives within us as will, were to receive the will of the other. We inwardly step over to the other person. It is as though we leave our body and enter into the body of the other. If this feeling increasingly takes the upper hand, if it spreads out lovingly to others as what I should like to call modern brotherly love, a real life-experience is engendered from this sharing in the will, in the entire soul-life of the other person. Many people could have this life-experience today were they not to let it become clouded by prejudices. Wherever it appears, it is rejected for reasons which are indeed not good. One needs only to recall a person like Lessing. At the end of his life, when all that he could bring forth by way of purely human greatness had passed through his soul, he wrote *The Education of the Human Race*, which culminates in his acknowledging the fact of repeated earthly lives. There are higher Philistines, just as there are blue stockings, and they have their judgements about such things. They say: yes, Lessing was a clever fellow throughout his life; but then he entered his

dotage and arrived at confused ideas such as that of repeated earthly lives.

But these repeated earthly lives are not a fictional idea;
they are what we experience if we do not confront another
person through a mere blood-relationship or some kind of
organic connection but if we are able truly to reach over to
what lives in his soul. Then we become completely absorbed in what is thrusting its way towards us — the spirit of
the one person is reaching over to the other person, and
from what he experiences in this way he is able to say: this
bond that has been formed for your soul and spirit with the
other person has not arisen through this life. Through this
life there has arisen what resides in the blood. But what
emerges as a necessity in the spirit has arisen through
something that has preceded this life. Anyone who really
traces these developments of the modern life of humanity
since the middle of the fifteenth century — and a mist is still
spread over these things as far as the majority of mankind is
concerned — will arrive at the idea of repeated earthly lives
by living together with other people. What manifests itself
in this way emerges something like a dream. I say 'like a
dream' for the following reason. When we go to sleep, we
enter an unconscious realm. Out of this unconscious realm
this or that emerges as a dream. This entering into the
unconscious in sleep can be compared with diving down
into the souls of our fellow human beings, as I have just
characterised it. Then out of this diving down there appears
out of this 'sleeping into' our fellows something like the
dream of repeated earthly lives — not pictorially but in a
very real sense; and this makes us aware that something of
this kind has to be sought if we are to find our way through
the world of the senses. And that which shines forth like a
dream out of social life becomes a complete certainty if we
cultivate the human will in the same way that I have previously described in the case of memory. But just as memory must become a fully conscious power, so must the will

for its part renounce something which entirely governs it in ordinary life.

What is it that governs our will, our wishes and desires in ordinary life? If our desires did not spring forth from the organic life of our body, the will would so to speak have nothing to do. Anyone who scrutinises the will in the light of experience knows that this will rests on our desires. But we can also free what works as the essential power of the will from our desires. To a certain extent we free it in social life. But this makes us begin to be aware of what really matters. We free it in social life through the fact that, when we love someone very close to us, when we immerse ourselves in such a person, we do not desire this person like a piece of meat. We love someone close to us not out of our desires; rather is there here an inclining of a desire-free will. But this desire-free will can also be cultivated through a particular training. This happens if we do not merely want what is to be obtained in the outer world — towards which one or another desire is directed — but if we incline our will towards our fellow human being and his development. This we can do. We all too often simply let life do this for us. But once one has outgrown school — that is, once one's education is no longer cared for by others — one can also cultivate an ongoing self-education, an ongoing self-discipline. We can take our own soul-being in hand, we can resolve to achieve this or that. If our lives have led us to a certain point, we can resolve to orientate ourselves in this or that sphere of life, to transfer our power of judgement to another area of life; in short, we can reverse our will. Whereas otherwise the will always works from within outwards, in the way that desires govern what is outside us, the will can be reversed, it can be directed inwards. In that we practise self-discipline through our will, in that we try to make ourselves better and better in one way or another, we are drawing upon that power of will which is free from desire. And what you find in my book *Knowledge of the Higher*

Worlds and in the second part of my *Occult Science* has — in addition to the other aims which I have already characterised — the intention that the individual should direct such a cultivating of the will towards himself, so that he increasingly — if I may put it like this — penetrates into himself with his will. But then if these two forces combine — the power of memory drawn forth from the unconscious which then takes hold of the human will — the individual will then know himself as a spirit, he will know that he has inwardly taken hold of the spirit in a purely spiritual way, he will know that he has not achieved this through the organs of the body. He will know about spiritual activity in the spirit, he will know what it means to say that soul and spirit are independent of the body.

9. *From:* The Human Soul in Relation to World Evolution, *GA 212, lecture of 27 May 1922*

(Translation revised from that of Rita Stebbing, published by Anthroposophic Press in 1984.)

It would not be right for modern man to seek this path into the spiritual world, a path which was appropriate in former times. He should not make the detour associated with the breathing but should follow the more inward path of thinking. Thus it is right today if, by concentrating his thoughts and thought-pictures in meditation, man transforms the otherwise merely logical connection between thoughts into something of a musical nature. Meditation today is in the first instance an experience in thought, a matter of making the transition from one thought into another, from one mental picture into another.

Whereas the yogi in ancient India passed from one kind of breathing to another, man today must try to enter livingly with his whole being into, for example, the colour red. Thus he remains within the realm of thought. He must then do the same with blue and he can experience the rhythm: red, blue; blue, red; red, blue and so on. This is a thought-rhythm, though not one which can be found in a logical thought sequence; it is a thinking that is much more alive.

If one perseveres for a sufficiently long time with exercises of this kind—the yogi, too, was obliged to carry out his exercises for a very long time—and really experiences the swing, rhythm and inner qualitative change between red and blue; blue and red; light and dark; dark and light: in short, if indications such as those given in my book *Knowledge of the Higher Worlds* are followed, the exact opposite is achieved to that of the yogi in ancient times. Instead of in a certain sense imbuing the functions of nerves and senses with breath, one *begins* with the nerves and senses and brings the processes associated with them into an inner swing, rhythm and qualitative change. The yogi blended thinking with breathing, thus turning the two processes into one. The aim today is to dissolve the last connection between breathing and thinking, which is in any case deeply unconscious. When in ordinary consciousness we think about our natural environment, the ideas that we form are never purely the product of our nerves and senses; a stream of breath is always flowing through this process. While we think, the breath continually pulsates through nerves and senses.

All modern exercises in meditation aim at entirely separating thinking from breathing. Thinking is not on this account torn out of rhythm; it is simply enabled to break free from an inner rhythm. Gradually, however, it is linked to an external rhythm. By setting thinking free from the rhythm of breathing we let it stream, as it were, into the rhythm of the outer world. The yogi withdrew into his own rhythm. Man today returns to the rhythm of the outer world. In *Knowledge of the Higher Worlds* you will find that one of the first exercises shows how to contemplate the germination and growth of a plant. This meditation sets out to free the picturing quality of thinking from the breath and to let it dive down into the growth-forces of the plant itself.

Thinking must reach out into the rhythm pervading the outer world. However, the moment when thinking really becomes free of the bodily functions, when it has been wrested away from the breath and gradually unites with the outer rhythm, it dives down — not into the sense-perceptible qualities of things — but into the spiritual aspect of individual objects.

We look at a plant: it is green and its blossoms are red. This our eyes tell us, and our intellect reflects about it. Our ordinary consciousness is based on such experiences. We develop a different consciousness when we separate thinking from breathing, when we connect it with what is outside us. This thinking learns to vibrate with the plant — how it grows, how it unfolds its blossoms, how in a rose, for example, green changes into red. Thinking vibrates right into the spiritual element which lies at the foundation of every single thing in the outer world.

This is how modern meditation differs from the yoga exercises practised in very ancient times. There are of course many intermediate stages; I simply mention these two extremes. I shall now indicate what happens when someone gradually enters into these outer rhythms.

The yogi sank down, as it were, into his own breathing process; he sank into his own self. In this way he experienced his own self as if in memory; he remembered what he had been before he came down to earth. We, on the other hand, in a soul sense leave our body and unite ourselves with what lives spiritually in the rhythms of the outer world. Through this means we are now able to *behold* what we were before we descended to the earth.

That, you see, is the difference. To illustrate it, I shall draw it schematically. Let this be the yogi [see over, first drawing, white lines]. He developed a strong feeling of his

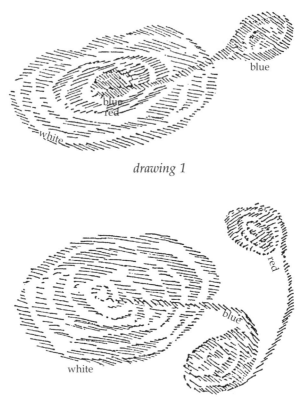

drawing 1

drawing 2

'I' [red]. This enabled him to remember what he was before he descended to the earth, when he was in a soul-spiritual environment [blue]. The stream of memory went back to the past.

Let this be the modern individual who has attained supersensible knowledge [second drawing, white lines]. He develops a process whereby he leaves his body [blue] and lives within the rhythm of the outer world; and he now *beholds* as an external object [red] what he was before he descended to the earth.

Thus at the present time a rightly developed under-standing of pre-birth existence is a direct beholding of what one was [red]. That is the difference.

10. From: *Mystery Knowledge and Mystery Centres, GA 232, lectures of 23 November and 9 December 1923*

(Translation revised from that by E.H.Goddard and D.S. Osmond, published by Rudolf Steiner Press in 1973.)

But you will be mistaken if you think that all you have to do is to look right or left, and that you will then see a shadowy form that is your astral body; that is not how things work. You must pay attention to what actually happens. Thus it could be, for example, that after such experiences you see the dawn very differently from hitherto. You will gradually begin to feel the warmth of the dawn as having a heralding quality, a natural pro-phetic power. You will begin to feel the dawn as some-thing spiritually forceful, and that there is some connection between that power and an inner sense within yourself; for although at first you may regard it as an illu-sion, you come to feel that there is some relationship between the dawn and your own being. Through such experiences as I have described, you will gradually come to feel as you look at the dawn: this dawn does not leave me alone. It is not merely there, and I am not merely here; I am inwardly connected with this dawn. It is a quality of my own soul; at this moment I am myself the dawn. And if you have been able to unite yourself with the dawn in such a way that you experience its coloured radiance — out of which the fiery ball of the sun pours forth its glory — so vividly that a sun rises from the dawn as a liv-ing experience in your heart, you will also gain the impression that you are travelling across the heavens with the sun, that the sun will not leave you alone, that it is not a case of the sun being there and you here but that in a sense your existence stretches right up to that of the sun—that in fact you are journeying through the day in company with the light.

If you develop this feeling not out of thinking but out of memory in the way I indicated, if you can develop these experiences out of the power of memory, you will find that the things which you have perceived with your physical senses acquire a different aspect; they begin to become transparent to the world of soul and spirit. Once you have gained the power of travelling with the sun in the dawn, all the flowers in the field will look different to you. The flowers do not merely display the yellow or red colours on their surface; they begin to speak spiritually to your soul. The flower becomes transparent; a spiritual element in the flower begins to stir and the blossoming becomes a sort of speaking. In this way you are actually uniting your soul with outer nature. You come to sense that there is something behind this nature, that the light with which you are connected is borne by spiritual beings. And in these spiritual beings you gradually recognise the characteristics described by anthroposophy.

9 December 1923
But as he [the pupil of the Hibernian Mysteries] moved towards the far distances of the blue ether, after the heights had uplifted him and carried him thither, he felt as though at the very end of the world of space something entered into him and vitalised him. This was what we today would call astrality, which was experienced inwardly and was far more intimately and forcefully united with man's being at that time, although it could not be perceived as strongly as is the case today. It was united with the human soul more forcefully and livingly than, though in a manner similar to, a feeling which

might arise within a person today if he were to expose himself to the instreaming, revivifying light of the sun to the point where it pervades him with an enlivening feeling of well-being in each of his organs. For if you expose yourself freely to the sun—though not to the point of inner discomfort—in such a way that you let its instreaming light and warmth bring a certain comfort to your body, you will without undue difficulty become aware of each individual organ in a different way from before. You come unmistakably into a condition where you can describe the very make-up of your organism.

If such things are so little known, this is due only to a lack in modern man's capacity to be genuinely attentive. Were this capacity not so lacking today, people would be able at least to give dreamlike indications of what is inwardly revealed to them in the instreaming sunlight. In earlier times, of course, the pupil was instructed about the inner constitution of the human organism quite differently from the way this is done now. These days people dissect corpses and make anatomical diagrams of them. This does not require much attentiveness, although it must be admitted that even this is not forthcoming from many students. But at all events, not much attention is required! In former times pupils of the Mysteries were taught by being exposed to the sun and were led to develop an awareness of their inner being as they reacted to the pleasant, instreaming sunlight; and afterwards they were well able to record their impressions of their liver, their stomach, and so on. This inner connection of man with the macrocosm can become a reality so long as the right conditions are established. You may be blind by nature and yet feel the form of an object by touching it. Similarly, when one of your organs is made sensitive to another through attentiveness to light, you can describe these inner organs at least in such a way that you can have a shadowy picture of them in your consciousness.

11. From: Mystery Centres of the Middle Ages, GA 233a, lecture of 13 January 1924

(Translation based on the third — revised — edition of that by Mary Adams, published under the title *Rosicrucianism and Modern Initiation* by Rudolf Steiner Press in 1982.)

The Copernican cosmology, for example, was taught in Rosicrucian schools; but in particular states of consciousness the ideas contained in it came back in the form I have explained to you. Indeed, it was the Rosicrucians who realised that what is learnt through modern knowledge must, so to speak, be offered up to the Gods, so that they may translate it into their language and give it back to man.

This possibility has remained up to the present time. For it is indeed the case, my dear friends, that if you, as people who are touched by the Rosicrucian principle of initiation, study the system of Haeckel with all its materialism, study it and at the same time fully apply the methods of cognition indicated in *Knowledge of the Higher Worlds*, if you learn about our human ancestors in Haeckel's *Anthropogenesis* (and in that form it may very likely repel you), learn all that modern science has to say about this subject, and then carry it towards the Gods — you will get what is related about evolution in my book *Occult Science*. Such is the connection between the feeble, shadowy knowledge that man can acquire here with his physical body and the knowledge the Gods can give him, if he first duly prepares himself by studying this external knowledge in the right spirit. But man must bring them what he can learn here on earth, for times have changed.

Something else has also happened. However much people today may try to create out of themselves in the way the old initiates did, they are unable to do so. The soul no longer transmits anything in the way it did for the old initiates. Everything becomes impure and riddled with instincts — as is evident in the case of spiritualistic mediums and in other morbid or pathological conditions. All that derives purely from within becomes impure; for the time for such creation is over and was actually already over in the twelfth or thirteenth centuries. What has happened can be expressed approximately as follows.

The initiates of the ancient Persian epoch inscribed a great deal into the astral light with the help of the resistance of the solid earth. When the first initiate of the ancient Persian epoch appeared, the whole of the astral light destined for man was like an unwritten slate. As I have told you, I shall speak later about the ancient Indian epoch; today I am going back only to the ancient Persian epoch. The whole of nature, all the elements — the solid, the liquid, the airy and the warm — were at this time an unwritten slate; and the ancient Persian initiates wrote as much as could be written on this slate by making use of the resistance of earth. This was how, to begin with, the secrets destined to come to man from the Gods were inscribed in the astral light. The tablet was inscribed to a certain degree, but to an extent it was still empty. The initiates of the Egypto-Chaldean epoch were then able to continue the writing in their way, arriving at their visions through the resistance of water. And so a second portion of the tablet was inscribed.

Then came the Greek initiates; they inscribed the third portion of the tablet. And so now the tablet of nature was fully inscribed. By the thirteenth or fourteenth century this was so. Human beings then began to write in the warmth ether, which becomes diffused. For a time — until the nineteenth century — they continued to write in the warmth ether; but they had no idea that this activity also appears in the astral light. However, the time has come when people must recognise that they cannot find the secrets of the world out of themselves in the old sense; rather should they be preparing themselves inwardly so that they can read what is now fully inscribed on the tablet. This is what we must prepare ourselves for today and develop the necessary maturity: that we no longer create out of ourselves like the old initiates but that we are able to read in the astral light what is written there. If we succeed in doing so, what we receive from the warmth ether will work as an inspiration through the Gods coming to meet us, bringing to us in its reality what we have acquired by our own efforts here on earth. And what we thus receive from the warmth ether exerts its influence in turn on all that stands written on the tablet through air, water and earth.

Thus the natural science of today is the true basis for spiritual seership. If one first learns through science about the properties of air, water and earth and acquires the necessary inner faculties, one finds that as one gazes into the elements of air, water and earth the astral light will stream forth — not like some vague mist or cloud but so that one can read in it the secrets of world-existence and human life.

What, then, do we read? We — the humanity of today — read what we ourselves have written in it. For what does it mean to say that the ancient Greeks, Egyptians, Chaldeans, Persians wrote in the astral light? It means that we ourselves have written it there in our former lives on earth.

You see, just as our memory, our inner memory of the ordinary things that we experience in ordinary life, preserves these things for us, so does the astral light preserve for us what we have written in it. The astral light is spread around us — a fully written tablet with respect to the secrets which we ourselves have inscribed. At the same time, this is what we must read if we would find the secrets again. It is a kind of evolution memory, which must arise again amongst mankind. An awareness must gradually develop that such an evolution memory exists, that humanity today needs to read in the astral light about its earlier cultural epochs in the same way that, at a later age in life, we read about our youth through our ordinary memory. It is because this needs to be brought to people's awareness that I gave the lectures here over Christmas. I wanted you to see that it really is a matter of drawing the secrets that we need today forth from the astral light. So the old initiation was directed mainly to the subjective life; the new initiation concentrates on the objective. That is the great difference. For all that is subjective, what the Gods have secreted in human beings, has been inscribed into the outer world. What they secreted in his sentient body came out in the ancient Persian epoch; what they secreted in his sentient soul came out during the Egypto-Chaldean period; what they secreted in his intellectual or mind soul came out during the Grecian epoch. But the consciousness soul which we are now to develop is independent; it brings forth nothing more out of itself. It stands over and against what is already there. As human beings we must find our humanity again in the astral light.

Source-Material by Other Authors

From: *Johann Wolfgang von Goethe,* The Theory of Colour, II*

S. 166. The after-image. Imagination. Memory of the sense of sight.

S. 167. The after-image must be clearly distinguished from the after-effect of being blinded. The after-image is held on to for longer only through free activity, and disappears as soon as the will lets it go, though the will can also call it forth again; the after-effect of being blinded hovers involuntarily before the mind, disappears and then reappears for objective reasons.

S. 168. The after-image is particularly alive where the soul's activity is intensified; whereas the after-effect of being blinded is generally sustained for longer in the case of a nervous disposition and asthenic condition, and disappears the quicker the more energetically life streams through the organ.

S. 169. I believe that as, after searchingly looking at the object, one holds on to the after-image longer and more concentratedly, it would through practice become possible to bring the after-image closer to the translucent reality of the archetypal picture, an exercise which would not be without its importance as a foundation for memory and the power of imagination.

S. 170. In connection with this, it can be maintained that memory and the power of imagination are active in the

---

*This work, originally published in 1810, was published in an English translation by Charles Lock Eastlake in 1840. This translation was re-issued by the M.I.T. Press, Cambridge, Massachusetts and London in 1970. However, the extracts quoted here were not included in this translation. [Translator]

sense-organs themselves, and that every sense has the memory and imaginative power peculiar to it which — as distinct and individual forces — are subjugated to the general power of the soul.

(There remains much that I could say about the potential of such inner images as have been called before my eyes. I had the gift that, when I closed my eyes and with my head lowered thought of a flower in the middle of my organ of sight, it did not linger for a moment in its original form but opened itself out and unfolded new flowers from both coloured petals and green leaves; they were not natural flowers but imaginary ones, though as regular as the rosettas of a sculptor. It was impossible to fix the creation that was streaming forth; nevertheless, it lasted as long as I wished, did not become exhausted or further intensified. I could evoke the same phenomenon if I thought of the orna-mentation of a brightly coloured disc, which likewise con-stantly changed from the middle towards the periphery, just like the kaleidoscope which has been invented in our own day. I do not recall to what extent a number was observable in the course of this regular movement, though probably it was related to the eightfold corolla, since the flowers spoken of above had no fewer petals than this. It did not not occur to me to make the attempt with other objects; the reason why these appeared so readily could well be that my many years of studying plant metamorphosis, together with my sub-sequent study of painted discs, had wholly imbued me with these objects; and this bears out Mr Purkinje's significant suggestion. Here we find after-image, memory, creative imagination, concept and idea manifesting themselves all at once in the independent vitality of the organ with total freedom and without intentionality or guidance.

The higher contemplaton of all the plastic arts is of direct relevance here; one can see more clearly the reason why poets and all true artists must be born. Their inner creative power has livingly to bring forth those after-images — the idols remaining behind in the organ, in the memory, in the power of imagination — voluntarily without intentionality and desire, they must unfold themselves, grow, spread out and draw together in order truly to change from shadowy abstractions into objective beings.)

From: *Manfred von Mackensen,* A Phenomena-based Physics*

After-Images and Contrast Phenomena

The perceptive activity of civilised people is largely a matter of merely responding to signals, a reflex to outwardly derived stimuli. In order that the pupils can find their way to a fulfilling experience of the world such as can make them inwardly rich, it is important at this age — when children are still so open to their senses — to cultivate by means of after-images, for example, a perception which concentrates the will but which also enhances the receptive listening faculties. Such a perception is developed if we do not — as we usually do — fix our gaze upon the edges of objects as if to bore into them with our eyes but, instead, become awake right into the far corners and look out into the surroundings, opening ourselves to the entire panorama

---

*These extracts derive from Manfred von Mackensen's *Klang, Helligkeit und Wärme*, published by the Pedagogical Research Department of the Union of German Waldorf Schools, Kassel 1988 (second edition 1992). An English translation — by John Petering — is published by the Association of Waldorf Schools of North America, Fair Oaks, California 1994. The translation offered here has been made with reference to this version.

The extracts are taken from the section about optics in class six (volume 1 of the English edition). The indications in this book are conceived of as working material for teachers and give us an insight into the way that children and young people in Waldorf Schools are made consciously familiar for the first time with the phenomenon of the 'after-image'.

and experiencing how all surfaces in the field of view stand in relation to each other. [...]

After-images (successive contrast) manifest the same counter-movement as images from the surrounding field of vision (simultaneous contrast): light becomes dark and vice versa. Complementary colours also reappear. Thus after-images arising from pale initial colours in a bright surrounding possess a magical, luminous light which depends only upon our vision and not upon external brightness; we are encountering a *colour-generating radiancy of the eye*. The pupils are very keen to see this often. One should try out an ascending sequence of such phenomena beforehand.

Coloured after-images (description of an experiment)

One of the many possibilities and variations is as follows. A piece of coloured paper (cardboard, crepe paper or cloth) of around chest size—it could be circular, triangular or star-shaped—is held in front of a brightly coloured wall or a white surface of some kind. After about 20 to 40 seconds of relaxed but fixed attention the coloured object is moved away, while one's attention continues to be directed towards the empty space: the complementary colour evoked (Goethe) can be seen in accordance with the form and size of the coloured surface which has been removed. The phenomenon becomes more radiant if the wall is illuminated throughout with something like an open slide-projector without a slide. On no account should one make the coloured surface *alone* very bright, such as through a coloured projection with coloured film and projector instead of a coloured paper on a bright wall.

More about after-images and colours

First we rest our gaze on a window-frame and a window-pane and then switch immediately to a medium grey surface; the previously dark forms appear bright and the bright dark. The eye responds to extremes with an equal-ising activity. One can, for example, make the experiment of holding a white card with a black triangle or something similar in front of a grey wall (or wrapping paper), and after quietly gazing at it taking it away—while continuing to look at the same spot. A dark rectangle with a light tri-angle appears. Both in looking at the strongly contrasted figure and in contemplating the after-image, it is essential not to try to survey and grasp what one sees in a repre-sentational sense but to dwell upon the whole panorama and pay attention to this—thus looking more at the whole field of vision rather than trying to identify the objects in it. For pupils who have difficulty in making themselves aware of the after-image, one could also begin with coloured objects.

The after-image is well known and usually has the status of a trivial, peripheral phenomenon of optics—in other words, something that is familiar but should be spurned as an illusion. This disdain is reasonable enough if we are not trying to go beyond merely stating that after-images exist; but there are two ways of going further.

One is to bring the will into perception. Reasoning activity, drawing conclusions about objects and other details, the ceaseless making of distinctions and mental acrobatics—all this must give way to a quiet, will-permeated contemplation of the after-image. The con-sciousness must be directed towards the qualitative and two-dimensional nature of seeing itself as an activity in its own right and not merely towards the multiplicity of objects. And if this is attempted on darker coloured surfaces (see the description of the experiment), one will be rewar-ded with the magically radiant colours of after-images—with the so-called complementary colours.

In addition to this training of the will in perception, after-images present us with a further exercise in thinking. What is actually being expressed in this inversion of light and dark and the engendering of complementary colours? If we look at the monotonous grey wall after the intense contrast between the window-frame and window-pane, our vision softens this abrupt change from high contrast to sameness by the after-image appearing on the wall. The highly contrasted image radiates something over the monotony of what is seen afterwards. However, the image interwoven with the monotonous aspect of the grey wall is not what was seen before but its light/dark- and its colour-complement (inversion). The pure contours, which are grasped by the sense of movement and its conceptual elaboration and not purely by seeing, remain unaltered whereas the brightness and colours of the surfaces appear transformed. This we owe to the quiet contemplation which has had an effect on our seeing as we studied the highly contrasted image (in the case of the window): the glaring brightness of the light parts becomes muted, while the dark parts become less black. This delicate moderation of contrast, which does not at first have anything to do with the after-image, can be directly observed. With slight movements of the eye, dark spots (for example) acquire a light edge; the after-image is already working in the initial image. This balancing out which occurs in the initial image during any quiet contemplation is already an interweaving of the light and dark parts; as the light becomes dark it undergoes modification and inversion. The after-image manifests this already existing tendency in an intensified form when one's eye is directed upon a surface lacking in contrasts. The contrast-moderating activity already mentioned develops further. The image towards which it was directed is now absent. Thus the continuing contrast-moderating activity creates a new complementary image which is an inversion of it. If, therefore, one focuses intensely on a deep green, one experiences this richness through the fact that one is already unconsciously creating red. Individual colours and individual states of brightness have—as we have seen—something unreal about them.

Repeatedly the question arises: are after-images real, or are they merely subjective? This question is inappropriately framed. What is supposedly subjective may have the greatest effects on the world and on the person experiencing it. It can therefore be regarded as real (as having an effect), even if it cannot be made manifest and grasped as an objectively separate entity. And moreover, after-images are never subjective in the sense of personal whims. Rather are they, in this respect, 'inter-subjective'.

However, nor, as said, are they wholly objective. They lack the second sense-quality [this was described earlier, and has to do with the sense of movement]. When in the course of creating the after-image, that is, in looking at the image in front of us, we keep our gaze fixed and so cut out the movement of our eyes, we bring about a visual impression (the subsequent after-image) which the sense of movement can no longer take hold of. For the after-image cannot be looked over or examined from different points of view with our eyes; with every movement of the eye it goes with it. By stripping away the second sense-quality, it renders it impossible to draw conclusions in the ordinary way about objects existing outside of us. We lose the sense of distance which the objective realm otherwise gives to our consciousness: the after-image accompanies us inescapably and fades involuntarily. It is not possible to turn away from one after-image to look at another.

We should leave the after-image in this state of delicate untouchability. To say 'It derives from the eye' would merely mean introducing the objective conclusion of another observer, on the grounds that we want to have objectivity at any cost. For the person seeing the after-image does not observe the organ of the eye; he only experiences the act of seeing.

The colour-laws of after-images give us Goethe's colour-circle. We find the order of the cold and warm colours. We are now able to study where the warm colours most characteristically occur in nature: in blood, in fire. There is much that can be linked in here. We could also develop a feeling for what the being of colour means altogether by observing initially grey, white, black and then coloured after-images. We can also gain a very clear experience of colour as a whole if we follow a path in the dim morning twilight and then shortly afterwards retrace it in the full light of day: we are astounded that we did not see all those beautiful colours the first time, and we can now compare in our mind a colourless and a coloured image of nature. Only with such observations do we arrive at the experience that a whole new realm of life is opened up to us through colour.

From: Agatha Christie, The Mysterious Mr Quin*

'A problem is not necessarily unsolvable because it has remained unsolved.'

'Oh! Come, man, if nothing came out at the time, it's not likely to come out now — ten years afterwards?'

Mr Quin shook his head gently.

'I disagree with you. The evidence of history is against you. The contemporary historian never writes such a true history as the historian of a later generation. It is a question of getting the true perspective, of seeing things in proportion. If you like to call it so, it is, like everything else, a question of relativity.'

Alex Portal leant forward, his face twitching painfully.

'You are right, Mr Quin,' he cried, 'you are right. Time does not dispose of a question — it only presents it anew in a different guise.'

---

*Originally published by Collins in 1930. The text is reproduced here in accordance with the paperback edition published by Harper Collins in 1993.

Evesham was smiling tolerantly.

'Then you mean to say, Mr Quin, that if we were to hold, let us say, a Court of Inquiry tonight, into the circumstances of Derek Capel's death, we are as likely to arrive at the truth as we should have been at the time?'

'*More* likely, Mr Evesham. The personal equation has largely dropped out, and you will remember facts as facts without seeking to put your own interpretation upon them.'
[...]

They sat in silence. Evesham brought his hand down with a bang on the table.

'Something must have happened in that ten minutes,' he cried. 'It must! But what? Let's go over it carefully. We were all talking. In the middle of it Capel got up suddenly and left the room—'

'Why?' said Mr Quin.

The interruption seemed to disconcert Evesham.

'I beg your pardon?'

'I only said: Why?' said Mr Quin.

Evesham frowned in an effort of memory.

'It didn't seem vital—at the time—Oh! of course— the Post. Don't you remember that jangling bell, and how excited we were. We'd been snowed up for three days, remember. Biggest snowstorm for years and years. All the roads were impassable. No newspapers, no letters. Capel went out to see if something had come through at last, and got a great pile of things. Newspapers and letters. He opened the paper to see if there was any news, and then went upstairs with his letters. Three minutes afterwards, we heard a shot ... Inexplicable—absolutely inexplicable.'

'That's not inexplicable,' said Portal. 'Of course the fellow got some unexpected news in a letter. Obvious, I should have said.'

'Oh! Don't think we missed anything so obvious as that. It was one of the Coroner's first questions. *But Capel never opened one of his letters.* The whole pile lay unopened on his dressing-table.'

Portal looked crestfallen.

'You're sure he didn't open just one of them? He might have destroyed it after reading it?'

'No, I'm quite positive. Of course, that would have been the natural solution. No, every one of the letters was unopened. Nothing burnt — nothing torn up. There was no fire in the room.'

Portal shook his head.

'Extraordinary.'

'It was a ghastly business altogether,' said Evesham in a low voice. 'Conway and I went up when we heard the shot, and found him — it gave me quite a shock, I can tell you.'

'Nothing to be done but telephone for the police, I suppose?' said Mr Quin.

'Royston wasn't on the telephone then. I had it put in when I bought the place. No, luckily enough, the local constable happened to be in the kitchen at the time. One of the dogs — you remember poor old Rover, Conway? — had strayed the day before. A passing carter had found it half buried in a snowdrift and had taken it to the police station. They recognised it as Capel's, and a dog he was particularly fond of, and the constable came up with it. He'd just arrived a minute before the shot was fired. It saved us some trouble.'

'Gad, that was a snowstorm,' said Conway reminiscently. 'About this time of year, wasn't it? Early January.'

'February, I think. Let me see, we went abroad soon afterwards.'

'I'm pretty sure it was January. My hunter Ned — you remember Ned? — lamed himself the end of January. That was just after this business.'

'It must have been quite the end of January then. Funny how difficult it is to recall dates after a lapse of years.'

'One of the most difficult things in the world,' said Mr

Quin, conversationally. 'Unless you can find a landmark in some big public event — an assassination of a crowned head, or a big murder trial.'

'Why, of course,' cried Conway, 'it was just before the Appleton case.'

'Just after, wasn't it?'

'No, no, don't you remember — Capel knew the Appletons — he'd stayed with the old man the previous spring — just a week before he died. He was talking of him one night — what an old curmudgeon he was, and how awful it must have been for a young and beautiful woman like Mrs Appleton to be tied to him. There was no suspicion then that she had done away with him.'

'By jove, you're right. I remember reading the paragraph in the paper saying an exumation order had been granted. It would have been that same day — I remember only seeing it with half my mind, you know, the other half wondering about poor old Derek lying dead upstairs.'

'A common, but very curious phenomenon, that,' observed Mr Quin. 'In moments of great stress, the mind focuses itself upon some quite unimportant matter which is remembered long afterwards with the utmost fidelity, driven in, as it were, by the mental stress of the moment. It may be some quite irrelevant detail, like the pattern of a wallpaper, but it will never be forgotten.'

'Rather extraordinary, your saying that, Mr Quin,' said Conway. 'Just as you were speaking, I suddenly felt myself back in Derek Capel's room — with Derek lying dead on the floor — I saw as plainly as possible the big tree outside the window, and the shadow it threw upon the snow outside. Yes, the moonlight, the snow, and the shadow of the tree — I can see them again this minute. By Gad, I believe I could draw them, and yet I never realized I was looking at them at the time.'

'His room was the big one over the porch, was it not?' asked Mr Quin.

'Yes, and the tree was the big beech, just at the angle of the drive.'

Mr Quin nodded, as though satisfied. Mr Satterthwaite was curiously thrilled. He was convinced that every word, every inflection of Mr Quin's voice, was pregnant with purpose. He was driving at something—exactly what Mr Satterthwaite did not know, but he was quite convinced as to whose was the master hand.

There was a momentary pause, and then Evesham reverted to the preceding topic.

'That Appleton case, I remember it very well now. What a sensation it made. She got off, didn't she? Pretty woman, very fair—remarkably fair.'

Almost against his will, Mr Satterthwaite's eyes sought the kneeling figure up above. Was it his fancy, or did he see it shrink a little as though at a blow. Did he see a hand slide upwards to the table cloth—and then pause.

There was a crash of falling glass. Alex Portal, helping himself to whisky, had let the decanter slip.

'I say—sir, damn' sorry. Can't think what came over me.'

Evesham cut short his apologies.

'Quite all right. Quite all right, my dear fellow. Curious—that smash reminded me. That's what she did, didn't she? Mrs Appleton? Smashed the port decanter?'

'Yes. Old Appleton had his glass of port—only one—each night. The day after his death, one of the servants saw her take the decanter out and smash it deliberately. That set them talking, of course. They all knew she had been perfectly wretched with him. Rumour grew and grew, and in the end, months later, some of his relatives applied for an exhumation order. And sure enough, the old fellow had been poisoned. Arsenic, wasn't it?'

'No—strychnine, I think. It doesn't much matter. Well, of course, there it was. Only one person was likely to have done it. Mrs Appleton stood her trial. She was acquitted more through lack of evidence against her than from any overwhelming proof of innocence. In other words, she was lucky. Yes, I don't suppose there's much doubt she did it right enough. What happened to her afterwards?'

'Went out to Canada, I believe. Or was it Australia? She had an uncle or something of the sort out there who offered her a home. Best thing she could do under the circumstances.'

Mr Satterthwaite was fascinated by Alex Portal's right hand as it clasped his glass. How tightly he was gripping it.

'You'll smash that in a minute or two, if you're not careful,' thought Mr Satterthwaite. 'Dear me, how interesting all this is.'

Evesham rose and helped himself to a drink.

'Well, we're not much nearer to knowing why poor Derek Capel shot himself,' he remarked. 'The Court of Inquiry hasn't been a great success, has it, Mr Quin?'

Mr Quin laughed...

It was a strange laugh, mocking—yet sad. It made everyone jump.

'I beg your pardon,' he said. 'You are still living in the past, Mr Evesham. You are still hampered by your preconceived notion. But I—the man from outside, the stranger passing by, sees only—facts!'

'Facts?'

'Yes—facts.'

'What do you mean?' said Evesham.

'I see a clear sequence of facts, outlined by yourselves but of which you have not seen the significance. Let us go back ten years and look at what we see—untramelled by ideas or sentiment.'

Mr Quin had risen. He looked very tall. The fire leaped fitfully behind him. He spoke in a low compelling voice.

'You are at dinner. Derek Capel announces his engagement. You think then it was to Marjorie Dilke. You are not so sure now. He has the restlessly excited manner of a man who has successfully defied Fate—who, in your own words, has pulled off a big coup against overwhelming odds. Then comes the clanging of the bell. He goes out to get the long overdue mail. He doesn't open his letters, but you mention yourselves that *he opened the paper to glance at the news*. It is ten years ago — so we cannot know what the news was that day — a far-off earthquake, a near at hand political crisis? The only thing we do know about the contents of that paper is that it contained one small paragraph — *a paragraph stating that the Home Office had given permission to exhume* the body of Mr Appleton three days ago.'

'What?'

Mr Quin went on.

'Derek Capel goes up to his room, and there he sees something out of the window. Sir Richard Conway has told us that the curtain was not drawn across it and further that it gave on to the drive. What did he see? What could he have seen that forced him to take his life?'

'What do you mean? What did he see?'

'I think,' said Mr Quin, 'that he saw a policeman. A policeman who had come about a dog — but Derek Capel didn't know that — he just saw — a policeman.'

There was a long silence — as though it took some time to drive the inference home.

'My God!' whispered Evesham at last. 'You can't mean that? Appleton? But he wasn't there at the time Appleton died. The old man was alone with his wife —'

'But he may have been there a week earlier. Strychnine is not very soluble unless it is in the form of hydrochloride. The greater part of it, put into the port, would be taken in the last glass, perhaps a week after he left.'

Portal sprang forward. His voice was hoarse, his eyes bloodshot.

'Why did she break the decanter?' he cried. 'Why did she break the decanter? Tell me that!'

For the first time that evening, Mr Quin addressed himself to Mr Satterthwaite.

'You have a wide experience of life, Mr Satterthwaite. Perhaps you can tell us that.'

Mr Satterthwaite's voice trembled a little. His cue had come at last. He was to speak some of the most important lines in the play. He was an actor now—not a looker-on.

'As I see it,' he murmured modestly, 'she cared for Derek Capel. She was, I think, a good woman—and she had sent him away. When her husband died, she suspected the truth. And so, to save the man she loved, she tried to destroy the evidence against him. Later, I think, he persuaded her that her suspicions were unfounded, and she consented to marry him. But even then, she hung back—women, I fancy, have a lot of instinct.'

Mr Satterthwaite had spoken his part.

Suddenly a long trembling sigh filled the air.

'My God!' cried Evesham, starting, 'what was that?'

Mr Satterthwaite could have told him that it was Eleanor Portal in the gallery above, but he was too artistic to spoil a good effect.

Mr Quin was smiling.

'My car will be ready by now. Thank you for your hospitality, Mr Evesham. I have, I hope, done something for my friend.'

They stared at him in blank amazement.

'That aspect of the matter has not struck you? He loved this woman, you know. Loved her enough to commit murder for her sake. When retribution overtook him, as he mistakenly thought, he took his own life. But unwittingly, he left her to face the music.'

'She was acquitted,' muttered Evesham.

'Because the case against her could not be proved. I fancy—it may only be a fancy—that she is still facing the music.'

Portal had sunk into a chair, his face buried in his hands.

Quin turned to Satterthwaite.

'Goodbye, Mr Satterthwaite. You are interested in the drama, are you not?'

Mr Satterthwaite nodded — surprised.

'I must recommend the Harlequinade to your attention. It is dying out nowadays — but it repays attention, I assure you. Its symbolism is a little difficult to follow — but the immortals are always immortal, you know. I wish you all goodnight.'

They saw him stride out into the dark. As before, the coloured glass gave the effect of motley. [...]*

'Well, Mr Quin?'

The latter shook his head.

'I'm not a magician. I'm not even a criminologist. But I will tell you one thing — I believe in the value of impressions. In any time of crisis, there is always one moment that stands out from all the others, one picture that remains when all else has faded. Mr Satterthwaite is, I think, likely to have been the most unprejudiced observer of those present. Will you cast your mind back, Mr Satterthwaite, and tell us the moment that made the strongest impression on you? Was it when you heard the shots? Was it when you first saw the dead bodies? Was it when you first observed the pistol in Mrs Staverton's hand? Clear your mind of any preconceived standard of values, and tell us.'†

From: Jacques Lusseyran, And There Was Light‡

It was a great surprise to me to find myself blind, and being blind was not at all as I imagined it. Nor was it as the people around me seemed to think it. They told me that to be blind

---

* Extract from the first story in *The Mysterious Mr Quin*.

† Extract from the second story in *The Mysterious Mr Quin*.

‡ Originally published in French in 1953. This translation, by Elizabeth R. Cameron, was first published in the United States in 1963. It was reissued by Floris Books in 1985.

meant not to see. Yet how was I to believe them when I saw? Not at once, I admit. Not in the days immediately after the operation. For at that time I still wanted to use my eyes. I followed their usual path. I looked in the direction where I was in the habit of seeing before the accident, and there was anguish, a lack, something like a void which filled me with what grown-ups call despair.

Finally, one day, and it was not long in coming, I realised that I was looking in the wrong way. It was as simple as that. I was making something very like the mistake people make who change their glasses without adjusting themselves. I was looking too far off, and too much on the surface of things.

This was much more than a simple discovery, it was a revelation. I can still see myself in the Champ de Mars, where my father had taken me for a walk a few days after the accident. Of course I knew the garden well, its ponds, its railings, its iron chairs. I even knew some of the trees in person, and naturally I wanted to see them again. But I couldn't. I threw myself forward into the substance which was space, but which I did not recognise because it no longer held anything familiar to me.

At this point some instinct — I was almost about to say a hand laid on me — made me change course. I began to look more closely, not at things but at a world closer to myself, looking from an inner place to one further within, instead of clinging to the movement of sight towards the world outside.

Immediately, the substance of the universe drew together, redefined and peopled itself anew. I was aware of a radiance emanating from a place I knew nothing about, a place which might as well have been outside me as within. But radiance was there, or, to put it more precisely, light. It was a fact, for light was there.

I felt indescribable relief, and happiness so great it almost made me laugh. Confidence and gratitude came as if a prayer had been answered. I found light and joy at the same moment, and I can say without hesitation that from that time on light and joy have never been separated in my experience. I have had them or lost them together.

I saw light and went on seeing it though I was blind. I said so, but for many years I think I did not say it very loud. Until I was nearly fourteen I remember calling the experience, which kept renewing itself inside me, 'my secret', and speaking of it only to my most intimate friends. I don't know whether they believed me, but they listened to me for they were friends. And what I told them had a greater value than being merely true, it had the value of being beautiful, a dream, an enchantment, almost like magic.

The amazing thing was that this was not magic for me at all, but reality. I could no more have denied it than people with eyes can deny that they see. I was not light myself, I knew that, but I bathed in it as an element which blindness had suddenly brought much closer. I could feel light rising, spreading, resting on objects, giving them form, then leaving them.

Withdrawing or diminishing is what I mean, for the opposite of light was never present. Sighted people always talk about the night of blindness, and that seems to them quite natural. But there is no such night, for at every waking hour and even in my dreams I lived in a stream of light.

From: Jacques Lusseyran, 'A New Vision of the World'*

Of course there are also eyes which feel as well as see. These are the eyes of a mother or of an anxious wife, the eyes of a

---

* *Ein neues Sehen der Welt.* As no English translation of this work is currently available, this brief excerpt has been translated from the German text.

good doctor, a wise person, an artist and—why not?—a comedian. But how is it that at this moment when the eyes see they seemingly become partly closed and turn their gaze inwards?

This process is called by many different names: reflecting, concentrating, thinking things over. If one thinks about it with any degree of precision, it becomes clear that it is always a defensive reflex to the act of seeing. Once we have taken in images by means of our eyes, we have a need also to give them substance, to fix and ground them in ourselves without any visual support, in a word, to give them an entirely new existence: inner existence. Without at least a temporary renunciation of this kind with regard to what our eyes convey to us, there can—so I believe—be no true knowledge. [...]

Everything carried on as if light were no longer this object of the outer world, no longer this strange source of illumination, no longer this phenomenon of nature which is sometimes there and sometimes not and over which we have so little power, but as if this light henceforth encompassed both the outer world and myself with a single movement, a single grasp.

When I was deprived of the light of my eyes, I could not say that the light that I saw came from outside. Just as little could I say that it came from within me.

And indeed: inner and outer have become inadequate concepts. When much later, during my studies, I heard people speak about the difference between objective and subjective, I was not satisfied: I saw too precisely that this difference is based upon a false notion of perception.

From: Alfred Heidenreich, The Vision of Christ in the Etheric World*

Remember that Rudolf Steiner speaks in those lectures†
about a movement of humanity into that sphere of the
clouds. Actually, the manifestation, the advent of Christ in
the etheric world is a meeting; the Christ, in His rhythmical
Presence, presses forward into the etheric sphere, into the
sphere of life, but humanity — and it is vital that Steiner says
'on its natural path of development'‡ — touches on that
sphere in its soul region. It is the first glimmering of an
awakening of new senses *which can see the etheric*. One might
think it is a first awakening of our etheric eyes. 'You see, we
think with our eyes,' he says; 'but we don't literally see with
the eyes we have in here' — and he pointed to his eyes. 'They
are a kind of microscope, or telescope, or camera, a fairly
dead body in us. We see by means of it, with etheric
activity.'§

He explains the physiologically perceived colours as the
result of etheric activity. If you look at green and afterwards
at a white sheet of paper you see red (literally, not in
anger!). This seeing red is due to the continuation of the
etheric activity of the eye, which answers to the impressions
of colours. We see a balance. We never see an actual colour
as it is, but always a balance. We produce complementary
colours through the etheric activity of our eye; and what we
see, the final physical effect, is a balance. Balance is so
deeply built into man that all our relationships are

---

* A lecture given — in English — to the Anthroposophical Society of
America in New York, 29 April 1949. Published under the title *The Risen
Christ and the Etheric Christ* by Rudolf Steiner Press in 1969.
† This refers to the lectures collected in GA 118, some of which are
published in English under the title *The Reappearance of Christ in the
Etheric*, Anthroposophic Press, New York 1983.
‡ Ibid., lecture of 25 January 1910.
§ Ibid.

balanced, or ought to be. (If you are sick, of course, your balance is disturbed.)

I have often wondered—and I say this with some caution because it is more an idea of my own—whether that very intensification of the natural etheric activity, to which we owe even our ordinary sense-perceptions, becomes more and more subtle, and more and more active. Some people, I realize, can experience that; for instance, the activity of the etheric eye before it enters fully into a physical instrument is one of the first things you can experience in the process of waking up. It is just here that the etheric body begins to awake, naturally, and it is the etheric forces which see. In his lectures *From Jesus to Christ*,* Steiner suggests that it is our own etheric activity which lightens up that sphere in which the Etheric Christ is present. In one sentence only he says this, but he does say it—that through our own activity we can shed some light. It is an activity which in its clarity, and beauty, can be strengthened through moral development; not necessarily only through the specific spiritual discipline of the meditative path, but really through moral development as a whole. That moral progress improves the etheric light we can shed from our own eyes, from our own heads, into the etheric world, to lighten up the Christ.

---

*GA 131. English translation published by Rudolf Steiner Press in 1973.

Baruch Urieli

Postscript

The Mystery of the After-Image

It is not easy to remember what is the complementary colour or after-image of a particular colour, though there is a simple rule which can be applied. If one thinks of the three primary colours of red, yellow and blue, the fact is that the complementary colour of red is green (i.e. blue and yellow). The complementary colour of yellow is red and blue (i.e. violet). The complementary colour of blue is red and yellow (i.e. orange). The circle of the primary colours is always closed in the after-image; the one colour calls forth the other two and vice versa. This is a fundamental law of the after-image.

Now there is a mysterious passage in the twelfth chapter of the Revelation of St John (12:3,4), where it says that the dragon casts one third of the stars down to the earth. What is this one third of the stars which are cast down? It is the world of maya, which we experience with our earthly senses. However, the after-image discloses to us the other two thirds that belong to it, which have remained in heaven.

Thus the world of the senses does not stand in contrast to the world of the spirit which it has lost but forms an indivisible unity with it, which remains hidden until the selfless self has learnt once again to perceive the spiritual two thirds missing from the earthly percept. In this way, it becomes possible for man to unveil the true meaning of existence, like a present-day pupil of Sais in Novalis's sense. With this the foundations can be created for a new Michael culture.